S0-BAV-117

Adventure on a **DARE**

Fritz T. Sprandel

With
Joshua E. Loomis
and
Dean A. Bartholomew

Illustrations by
Linda M. Heberling

authorHOUSE®

AuthorHouse™
1663 Liberty Drive
Bloomington, IN 47403
www.authorhouse.com
Phone: 1-800-839-8640

© *2009 Fritz T. Sprandel. All rights reserved.*

No part of this book may be reproduced, stored in a retrieval system, or transmitted by any means without the written permission of the author.

First published by AuthorHouse 8/3/2009

ISBN: 978-1-4389-5662-6 (sc)
ISBN: 978-1-4389-5663-3 (hc)

Printed in the United States of America
Bloomington, Indiana

This book is printed on acid-free paper.

To Robert Bell —
— Thank you —
10/26/10

LINDA M HEBERLING 04

v

Contents

Dedication

This book is dedicated to all those living and dead who have been a blessing to me not only in my travel and adventure, but also throughout all my life experience.

To those living, may they know of my deep appreciation for all they have done for me no matter how great or small their efforts.

And to all those who have passed on, may their spirit of care for their fellow man continue to live and touch the hearts of others and bless the heart of God.

I also want to thank Josh Loomis, coauthor; Dean Bartholomew, editor; and Linda Heberling, illustrator, for their generous, expert help.

Introduction

The first day I met Fritz Sprandel, I knew he would be a friend for life. He has a disarming, engaging way about him.

We met on a winter morning a few years ago outside the service entrance of a multi-franchise car dealership in Emmaus, Pennsylvania. Fritz came out into the cold, fresh air and started up a conversation with me. He was waiting for service to be completed on his Buick Regal and didn't want to sit cooped up in the dealer's waiting room with an unavoidable TV blaring. I soon learned how much he loved fresh air!

I had been hired part time by the service manager to help direct traffic because the owners had just added another franchise to their lineup and people were confused about where to pull in for service. Fritz asked me if I had done this as my career—wear a baseball cap bearing a bright orange and black logo and wave to customers at an auto service entrance.

I took no offense at Fritz's question. He didn't know me; he was just trying to strike up a friendship. I explained that I had retired from a thirty-year career as a typographer, proofreader, copy editor, and writer, and that I was now just enjoying a fun job in the great outdoors involving my favorite pastime—cars.

When I mentioned I was a retired writer, Fritz perked up. He told me he was looking for someone like me to help him organize his memoirs into a book about the adventures he had taken when he was younger. When Fritz told me a few details about his amazing solo canoe journey, I was immediately hooked and assured him I could help him with the project. A few days later he gave me his typewritten manuscript, and as I typed the story on my computer, I worked my copy editing magic. (Fritz has more courage than writing ability.)

The more I read about the experiences Fritz describes in his journals, the more intrigued I became. I found especially exciting the story of how he was captured by Cuban soldiers, the truth about the Americans he met in the Cuban prison where he was detained, and how he managed to emerge alive from a trial by Fidel Castro's Revolutionary Tribunal.

Any doubts I had about the veracity of his claims evaporated when I read the magazine and newspaper articles published when he was on his incredible journeys. A little research on the Internet provided even more documentation of Fritz's jaunts, which I incorporated into his stories, and I handed the finished product back to my fearless new friend.

When I inquired a few weeks later whether he liked what I had done with his memoirs, to my surprise, Fritz reported that the editing looked good, but as he reviewed all the facts of his encounters, he suddenly found himself on a search for the deeper meaning of his life. He wanted to find out why he had been preserved through all his challenges. I happily assured Fritz, a recovering alcoholic, I could help him on this quest as well.

Josh Loomis then took over on the project and helped Fritz recall even more memories as he reflected on his treks. Josh's incredible talent for adding color and improving the descriptions of some of the harrowing experiences Fritz endured and survived helped Fritz realize it was probably Providence that had preserved him.

This book is the result of Fritz's newfound passion to share his tales of derring-do and his interaction with the intriguing people he met along the way. It is the last item on Fritz's "bucket list." He has done almost everything the rest of us only dream of doing!

— Dean Bartholomew, Editor

Prologue

I've never met a man like Fritz Sprandel. I'd be hard-pressed to name someone who epitomizes the American archetype more than Fritz. He's been a farmhand, a wanderer, an explorer, an adventurer, and even a prisoner of a foreign power that suspected him of being an American spy. But these are things Fritz has done. What might not come across in the riveting story that follows on these pages is the kind of man Fritz Sprandel is.

I met Fritz on several occasions after I first encountered him in one of my father's Bible study groups. The first thing that struck me about him was his down-to-earth attitude and gregarious nature. He was always ready with a handshake and a smile, wondering how things were going, and willing to lend a compassionate ear. For a while I considered him another friendly face in that group. That was before Fritz began to tell me some of his stories, which strained credulity at first. Had this rather soft-spoken senior citizen really traveled so many miles, weathered so many storms, and encountered so many people?

But as time went on, the more stories Fritz told me and the more articles I read in research to help Fritz tell his astounding tale of adventure, survival, and mistaken identity, the more I began to understand how the bold and seemingly careless man who'd been called "Fearless Fritz" had become the man who sat across from me at the local restaurant where we met on several occasions.

The experiences that follow, both in these pages and beyond, helped shape Fritz even though he'd already been through quite a bit in his life. He learned a great deal in his journeys—more than he expected. Fritz didn't set out on these journeys to make history or to discover himself or to gain future fame or fortune. He did these things because he could. It is this spirit, this very American sense of freedom, that made Fritz fearless then and makes him the guide and friend that he is today.

Very few people I have met embraced this liberty in the way Fritz did. And while some of the risks he took were dangerous and, on more than one occasion, not terribly bright, he did everything with a zest for life and unflappable gusto that is worthy of the great frontiersmen of our country and adventurers the world over. It is my sincere hope that as you turn the page to begin Fritz's unforgettable journey, you will not only enjoy following him on every twist and turn his path takes, but will also learn something about yourself and challenge yourself to embrace the spirit of liberty that dwells within all of us. You don't have to be an adventurer, an explorer, an astronaut, or even an American spy to be as fearless as Fritz. You just have to seize the opportunities that come your way and let yourself be who you want to be, even if it scares you. After all, it's only in embracing our fears that we become truly fearless.

—Josh Loomis, Coauthor

"Adventurer"
What you do today
is harder than yesterday,
but easier than tomorrow.
SO DO IT!

Fritz, 2/7/2008

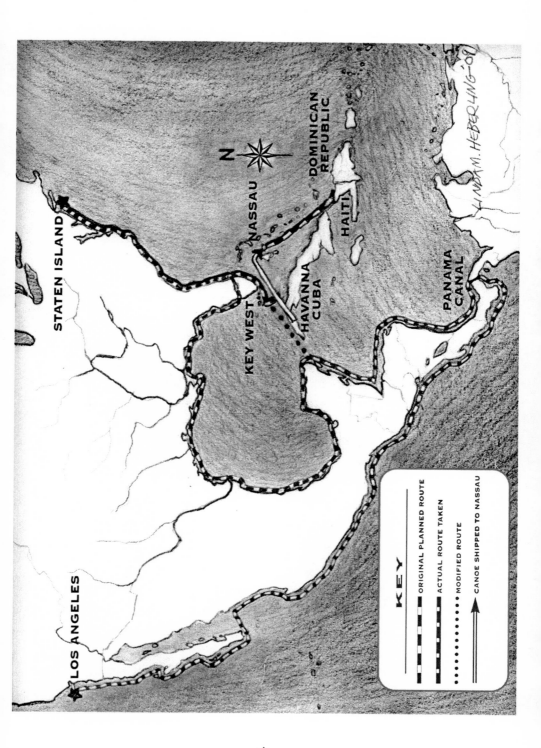

KEY
ORIGINAL PLANNED ROUTE
ACTUAL ROUTE TAKEN
MODIFIED ROUTE
CANOE SHIPPED TO NASSAU

LOS ANGELES
STATEN ISLAND
KEY WEST
NASSAU
HAVANNA
CUBA
HAITI
DOMINICAN REPUBLIC
PANAMA CANAL

N

ADAM. M. HEBERLING '09

FRED B. ROONEY
MEMBER OF CONGRESS
15TH DISTRICT, PENNSYLVANIA

COMMITTEE:
INTERSTATE AND
FOREIGN COMMERCE

SUBCOMMITTEE:
COMMUNICATIONS AND POWER

Congress of the United States

House of Representatives

Washington, D.C. 20515

October 9, 1970

Morris Perkin, Esquire
Perkin, Twining, Webster & Christie
516 Commonwealth Building
Allentown, Pennsylvania 18101

Dear Morris:

I was pleased to receive your letter regarding
the adventure of Fritz Sprandel and your personal role
in making arrangements for his travel documents and
Panama Canal passage.

Requests such as yours add a bright interlude to
the monotony of many of the more routine requests which
cross my desk. Frankly, I was totally unaware of the
procedures to be following in traversing the canal and
I find the request an opportunity to learn something totally
new.

My office today contacted the Secretary of the
Panama Canal Company, W. M. Whitman, and was assured of
assistance to solve the problems. A letter outlining
the details of Mr. Sprandel's trip and several newspaper
clippings are being forwarded now for Mr. Whitman's
attention.

Briefly, the requirements involve presenting evidence
of citizenship and of ownership or registration of the
"vessel." There is some question whether any proof of
ownership or registration will be required for a canoe.

It is my understanding that the documents are
presented to the Port Captain at the Atlantic end of the
canal. He, in turn, arranges for passage through the
canal. Occasionally, and this I believe would conflict
with Mr. Sprandel's objective, small boats such as "row-
boats" are required to be taken aboard larger vessels
for the trip through the locks.

There also are requirements about taking aboard a pilot and linesmen--enough manpower to get the boat through the locks safely if there are not enough personnel aboard--which apparently are flexible enough to be optimistic about accommodating Mr. Sprandel's objective to make the trip under his "own steam."

"We have even had people swim through," the Panama Canal Company advised. They were most willing to cooperate and gave assurances that they feel all possible problems can be worked out satisfactorily. Therefore, as soon as I receive further word, I will advise you. Also, in response to your question, I would have no objection to your publicizing the efforts to arrange passage. In fact, I got the distinct impression the Panama Canal Company, itself, is interested in the novelty of the adventure and its news value.

With kind personal regards, I am

Sincerely yours,

Fred B. Rooney, M.C.

FBR:cse

Chapter 1: **Fog and Fishermen**

I gave a wave to friends' and reporters' cameras alike, and pushed the *P.S. Enterprise* into the tidewaters washing against the dock. It hit me: I was really doing it. I looked out over the vast Hudson Bay. Taking a deep breath, I dipped my paddle into the water, nudging the canoe out into the bay.

Both the bay and my life were devoid of markers or signposts pointing the way. At any juncture, I could get lost or cast into the unknown by the capricious hand of fate. But right then, I felt I was fully in control, and no matter what the odds might be I could beat them. I had no idea how wrong I was.

My sense of foreboding grew as I embarked. Oppressive eighty-degree temperatures, humidity, and ominous, smoke-colored clouds on the horizon seemed to warn me not to go. But I summoned all the courage I had and pushed further out into the water. Leaving my friends' cheers behind me, I paddled southeast into five- to ten-mile-per-hour winds.

After only an hour on Hudson Bay, I encountered my first obstacle: a thick wall of fog, as gray as the hull of a battleship and almost as intimidating. And it was moving in my direction. I was going to have to decide quickly if I should brave the fog or turn the *P.S. Enterprise* around.

Unfortunately, however, the decision was about to be made for me. A small speedboat pulled up beside me. Riding in the back was a TV reporter and his cameraman.

"Nasty fog bank," the boat pilot said, following my gaze.

The reporter pointed, turned to me, and shouted out, "You want to come back with us, Fritz? Nobody would blame you, considering this soup."

I couldn't deny how scary the fog looked. But I was in the water now; the ocean lay before me, although I couldn't see further than a few dozen yards. I'm not sure what other people would've done in my position, but I wasn't about to chicken out this early. In fact, I wasn't planning to back out at all. I conjured up in my mind the subtle looks of disappointment sure to show up on my friends' faces if I came back on shore. I could hear them telling me how I was brave for trying, and this was something I didn't want. They didn't understand that now, more than anything else, I wanted to achieve my goal. Besides, Andy had given me two days; I had to at least do that.

I gave the reporter a friendly glance. "Thanks, but no thanks. I've got a long way to go. If I let a little foggy patch slow me down, I won't get anywhere."

They wished me luck and headed back to shore. I kept the *Enterprise* oriented toward the southeast and paddled straight into the fog. It wrapped around me. Silence. I began to wonder if maybe I should've let the TV crew tow me back to shore after all.

The fog was so thick I couldn't see a thing in front of my canoe. I'd dealt with fog like this before, but like most people, I'd done it in a car. Anybody who's driven through thick fog can tell you it's a disorienting experience, to say the least. Landmarks familiar in any other weather become meaningless. You drive, led forward only by the dotted line in the center of the road.

Now take away the line. Then take away the road. I felt like I was in a haunted house. I was scared because I had no idea what would happen to me next.

I'd seen buoys scattered around before I'd started out, but now I couldn't see a single one of them. I could hear their bells, however. I also heard the bellowing of horns on much larger ships in the bay—ocean liners and big freighters, no doubt—and the soft murmur of traffic in the vague direction of the city. The bow waves and powerful wake-generated swells lifted my canoe and me out of the water several times, as if a great, unseen hand were pushing me around. To this day I can't recall a time I was more unsettled.

- Lost in the mist -

I had no idea where I was in the bay, and I was starting to think coming out this far first was a bad idea. I told myself I should've kept to the shoreline, hugging the coast and not risking conditions like this. I paddled the *Enterprise* in the direction I felt was most likely south and knew the safety of shore could not be far. I could hardly tell if it was still daylight or not. I'd set out from the beach in the middle of the afternoon, but now it looked more like night. I told myself I wasn't tired, but my arms were so difficult to lift, the paddle felt like it was made of lead. The sounds of traffic didn't seem to be coming any closer. A soft, steady rumble in the distance and the quiet splashing of my paddle in the water were the only sounds.

Then the chilling calm was broken by a loud horn directly to my right. I was so startled I instinctively threw my arms up toward the blast, and my paddle struck metal. Then the "flight" aspect of my fight-or-flight reflexes took over, and I pushed with all my might away from the huge unknown object. The *Enterprise* slipped away from what I soon discovered was the hull of a ship, and I looked up. My neck craned as my eyes kept moving skyward, and the canoe buffeted further back. It must have been a commercial freighter. The behemoth would have plowed me under if her pilot hadn't hit the horn at exactly the right moment.

I know the crew gave me about as much notice as I would have given an ant accidentally encountered with my foot during a walk down a busy street. I had no reason to call out to them, and besides, my heart was pounding far too fast to think about telling them to watch where they were going. Death was knocking at my doorstep, and I had only been out for an hour.

Terror sank cold claws into my heart. The next time I might not be so lucky to hear the warning of Gabriel's horn. I had to focus. I knew this was the first obstacle of many I would encounter in this DARE. I found myself saying, "Sit upright. Relax the shoulders. Make steady, deliberate strokes with the paddle." I was quietly repeating the directions I'd given my canoeing students at a summer camp years ago. A small voice inside my head told me I really should rethink the trip. I told myself out loud, "No!" in response, finding comfort in the sound of a human voice among the horns and sounds of massive ships, which more than once had made me almost jump out of the *Enterprise*. It took me a long time to calm down.

Then I heard the first roll of thunder.

I clenched my teeth, snarled out a curse, and paddled still harder. But I couldn't outrun the storm. Bright, jagged bolts of lightning stabbed down through the fog, and before I knew it rain was coming down in sheets. The *Enterprise* began taking on water. In a flash I had my wet sneakers off, using them to bail out my vessel as quickly as possible. The terror now crawled around in my stomach, a caged jungle cat waiting to pounce. I was about to start paddling again when something slammed into my canoe.

- The fisherman in the fog -

For a brief, panic-filled moment, I imagined something titanic had hit me under the pitch-black sky. But it was merely a small rowboat. The fisherman inside was swathed in the yellow overcoat and hat of a man accustomed to fishing in bad weather. He spat seawater over the other side of his boat and grinned at me.

"Fine day for fishin', eh?" he shouted. His oars were secured to the aluminum hull with large, sturdy rings, and he was using a net to fish at the moment. He also had a large lamp perched on the stern of his boat. He looked me over—my waterlogged shoes and my swamped canoe.

"Be better for canoeing if it wasn't raining!" I yelled back over the storm. He laughed.

"Well, I must say," he continued to shout out, "I'm surprised to see you in this water with that kind of boat! It's only wood and canvas, son! But never mind it now. You can save your arms some trouble at the moment, because the tide's doing some work for you. It's coming in now, pushing us away from this nasty squall. You've got to know when the tide's going in and out."

"It would be helpful to have a radio," I responded meekly.

"Can't depend on them—Mother Nature's got a habit of short-circuiting the blasted things," he informed me. "You've got to learn by feel. Old fishermen's trick."

I nodded. He continued to teach me about boating in tidewaters, hanging over the side of his boat, keeping the *Enterprise* close and answering my questions. Soon the rain began to slow up a little bit. It was as if the ocean were quieting down so both it and I could hear this seasoned veteran of the sea. His jovial nature rubbed off on me, and I found myself less downcast about my condition. He looked over my canoe again.

"One thing you always have to remember is safety," he advised. "Can't stress it enough. You see my boat, here? Everything is secured in case I get capsized, and I have this lantern for days like today. Here, let me give you a spare torch." He leaned over and produced a sturdy D-cell flashlight with a metal body, which we tied to the stern of the canoe. "There! Now you've got a stern light. What's it going to help you do, now?"

"Stay safe?" I ventured. He grinned and patted my shoulder.

"There you go," he said like a special education teacher satisfied with his remediation. "Now, stay with this tide. It's going to take you in close to shore. When the fog lifts, the tide should be going out, and you can head out again. How far are you going?"

"I was planning on stopping at Sandy Hook," I answered. "It's the first of many stops. This little canoe and I are going all the way to California. We're going to head down along the Atlantic coastline, all the way around Florida, up around the panhandle of Florida, past the states bordering the Gulf of Mexico, around the Yucatan Peninsula in Mexico, down to Central America and through the Panama Canal."

He whistled. "You just woke up this morning and felt like taking a trip?"

"Actually, my friend dared me I couldn't do it," I explained. "He bought all my equipment, and gave me a dime to call him when I chickened out."

"Some friend!" he snorted.

I shrugged and produced a couple beers out of the ice chest and handed one to the fisherman. He took it happily. "Okay, I take it back," he said with a laugh. "If he sent you out with booze and made sure you had water to prepare food, he can't be all bad. Let's drink these once we reach the shore. The fog and storm will make bigger fools of us if we get drunk out here."

We were both working as hard as we could now to move our vessels through the water, and finally the shore came into view. I landed and looked around. Some weathered signs along the beach told me I was somewhere in the Atlantic Highlands of New Jersey, only a few miles from Staten Island. Sandy Hook Bay was still miles away, I thought to myself as I set about emptying the canoe and dumping the rest of the rainwater out by tilting it upside down. For now I was safe. The fisherman landed and did a little bailing as well and then looked to his catch.

While I was debating if I should rest more or give up and head back to Allentown, the faces of my friends came to me again, and I knew I didn't have the guts to admit defeat. The rain stopped quite suddenly, and the water became so calm it seemed as if the storm had never happened. And by now, the fog was not quite as thick as before, and I could see for about a quarter of a mile. It was time to move on.

Soaked sneakers, I found out the hard way, don't make for terribly good traction on the sand, but the *Enterprise* slipped back into the water without too much effort, and I resumed my course. My confidence swelled because I knew I could see much farther now. I took my time, however, remembering the fisherman's lessons on staying safe when navigating tidewaters, and giving my arms a chance to relax after the frantic paddling during the storm.

After a few hours I arrived at Atlantic Highlands in Sandy Hook Bay, which was easy to pick out, thanks to the Twin Lights Lighthouse I could see off in the distance. The sun had slipped down far to the west and the fog had cleared enough to let shafts of light from the full moon overhead reach down onto the water's surface. After the terror and savagery of the afternoon, the peaceful beauty of the evening was a welcome and serene sight, but I was far too tired to pull out my camera. All I could do was gratefully enjoy the gift of this panorama as I turned my canoe back to shore again.

I could see the lights of New York City reflecting clear across the bay. It was a strange feeling, sitting there wondering what millions of city people were doing under those lights—and me now safe and all alone. Landing, I dragged the canoe farther up from the shoreline and took some time to write in my logbook. I unrolled my sleeping bag, lay looking at the stars, thinking how lucky I was to be alive. Relaxing, I soon dozed off.

Something woke me only a few minutes later. I had the distinct feeling I was being watched. I sat up and saw a figure approaching me along the beach. It was a casually dressed man, and he smiled and waved.

"There you are!" he exclaimed. "I got a call from a friend of mine up near Staten Island who said you'd be down this way with an old flashlight of his, and you might be looking for some refreshment."

Another fisherman, he carried a steel thermos, and from it poured me some hot coffee. We talked for a while about tidewaters and navigating the ocean without anyone accompanying me. Then he advised me to leave around 5 a.m. in order to take advantage of those tides, and helped me settle in for the night. After a beer and a swig of Dewar's, I began to doze off. Somewhere halfway between dozing and sleeping soundly, I reviewed in my mind the events leading up to the dare.

Chapter 2: **Andy Perkin's Dare**

I remembered the Apollo 13 astronauts had made it back to earth after their dangerous flight around the moon. Regular gas was selling for thirty-six cents a gallon. Pay phone calls were ten cents. The Kent State shooting had drawn one hundred thousand people to march on Washington protesting the National Guard action, the Vietnam War, and President Nixon's invasion of Cambodia. The year was 1970.

Like many of my adventures and dares, it all started in a bar. I had good friends, a little to drink, a day with no responsibilities, and no common sense.

I had nothing holding me back from doing what all the rest of you laugh about over your beer or Scotch on the rocks before you go back to your wife, your job, your mortgage, and the masters you must obey every day.

This is one of those adventures, and it started on bravado and a huge dare on one thin dime.

I really didn't plan beforehand that my trip would include a Cuban jail with Black Panthers, a Communist leader, and a Revolutionary Tribunal trial.

On a typical drinking day in August I sat at Ye Old Ale House in Allentown, Pennsylvania, watching Walter Cronkite anchor the news on TV, the way I did so many nights back then, in a drunken haze. The Ale House was rather busy, and in a nearby corner booth someone was telling a joke about all the airplane hijackings to Cuba over the past three years, calling it Cuba's top sport. Andy Perkin sat beside me that August night, rambling on like he often did, commenting on Cronkite's reporting skill and taking great delight in disparaging my favorite sport, canoeing.

- The dare at the bar -

"Fritz, you couldn't get a canoe down a river like the Mississippi or the Delaware," Andy said, rattling the ice in his Scotch as he sat beside me. "One bad storm, and you'd be sunk."

I held up my bottle of beer, ordering another. "If a canoe is water-worthy, it's river-worthy," I insisted, setting my beer back down. "Hell, maybe even seaworthy."

Andy laughed. "I'd undoubtedly pay to see this. You, an amateur navigator at best, taking a canoe into the open ocean?"

My curiosity immediately went into overdrive when he brought up the subject of money. My lifestyle was not producing large sums of income, and at the age of twenty-five I had no savings.

"You'd pay, eh?" I asked. "How much?"

He looked at me in disbelief, and then emptied his Scotch in one gulp. "You're serious!"

"I wouldn't cross the Atlantic; that's just plain crazy," I told my friend with a grin. "But how about, say, New York to LA by way of the Panama Canal?"

Andy blinked, then burst out laughing again. "Okay, Fritz, you're on!" He slammed his glass down. "I'll give you what you need—and the only cash you get is a dime, to call me when you decide to give up and come home. My guess? Two days, tops."

I laughed it off. My interest faded when the only money mentioned was ten cents. And yet I felt an overwhelming impulse deep inside telling me maybe this was my chance to do something unique with my aimless life, with or without any immediate financial reward. I had the skills, strength, and energy to paddle a canoe. What the heck, I spent most of my summers working on the waterfront at two camps on the Delaware River giving others canoeing lessons.

We made jokes about mermaids and sea monsters at the bar until last call, and then ambled off in our separate directions.

The next morning's brilliant sunrise brought with it the inevitable hangover, aggravated by the ringing phone. The caller was an excited, inquisitive reporter from *The Morning Call* who wanted the know the route of my trip, how long I calculated it would take, what supplies Andy would be giving me—then I remembered the night before.

Had I really said I'd canoe from New York to LA through the Panama Canal? I answered the reporter's questions the best I could and then called Andy. He was on his way to the Army & Navy Store, he informed me, to pick up supplies for me. I told him I'd meet him there.

This wasn't the first time I'd done something on a dare. The first time, I'd hitchhiked across the United States with nothing but a single dollar bill and six Oreo cookies in my pocket. I can't recall why I did it, other than someone suggested I couldn't. That situation was different, though. Back then I had CJ in my life. I had come back from the service a few years before, glad to have survived, but disappointed in the lack of contact from my family. The one letter I'd sent to my mother to tell her I loved her and that I missed my family while overseas she returned to me covered in red-pen corrections and graded "D+" as if I were one of her English students. Needless to say, it was the last letter I wrote her—or anybody else, for that matter.

The first time I met CJ, I could tell she was special. I told her so, and then I kissed her and told her I was going to marry her. I courted her the best way I knew how, sometimes sleeping under her bedroom window merely to be near her. This was long before things like "stalkers" and "restraining orders" were in the common parlance, but CJ didn't mind at all, and neither did her family—we got along fine. I ended up working for her father after our marriage, and we moved into a rather upscale house.

A couple of years later, in mid-April of 1967, CJ and I were on a motorcycle ride through Allentown. I remember clearly a car making a left turn right in front of us, and we had no time to stop or swerve. I don't remember much after the impact.

At first the ambulance crew thought I was dead, CJ told me later. I'd gone through the car headfirst without a helmet. They were working on CJ when they saw me move, and so they quickly pulled me from the wreckage. CJ was lucky, escaping with only a couple broken ribs. I, however, needed more care. In fact, I established the record for the longest stay in the Intensive Care Unit at Allentown General Hospital. I was in a cast from head to toe; my jaw was broken in seven places, and when the accident came up in court the judge wouldn't allow some of the photographs to be shown to the jury because he deemed them "too graphic and gory."

When I was finally free of the hospital and the cast, I had little pain medication and no support from or contact with my own family. My mother didn't care if I was alive or dead. CJ tried to be there for me, but she was also trying to heal her own injuries. My only friend seemed to be my evening drink. At first, one beer seemed to help me get to sleep at night. Eventually one beer was not enough, and so I had two. Then two beers became four and soon four became eight. When I woke up one morning on a pile of laundry bags in the basement of the Laundromat next door to my favorite bar with the case of beer bottles I'd emptied the night before scattered around me, I couldn't deny it any longer—I was a drunkard.

Things went downhill with CJ. She pleaded with me to stop drinking. I couldn't. Finally, her patience wore out and she left me. To this day, I try not to think too much about what I've lost. My drinking led to a separation, and the separation led to more drinking.

- I get my equipment -

I was sober when I got to the Army & Navy Store, although sobriety at this point was far from a credo. Andy was in the parking lot, lashing a modest wood-and-canvas canoe to the roof of his car. He was concentrating on the knots, but I was examining the vessel. It seemed sturdy enough for a jaunt across a lake or down a few miles of river, but I was uncertain of its seaworthiness, despite the heated debate of the night before. I wasn't about to back out, however.

After a long moment, Andy turned and caught sight of me. "There you are," he said with a grin. "Don't worry, I already got you plenty of beer. And I threw in a bottle or two of Dewar's—don't say I never gave you anything. You want to pick out your MREs?"

"MREs? I'm taking Army sea rations?"

"I thought after your time in the Service you'd have gotten used to good old U.S. Army–issue Meals-Ready-to-Eat. They've got a good selection for you. We'll also want to make sure you have a good container for fresh water."

"Why's that, if I have beer?"

"Well, you can't make MREs with seawater, and I don't think Dewar's and seawater would taste that good," he replied as we walked into the store. The aforementioned booze would be held in an ice chest we picked out, a modest one, leaving room in my canoe for a second good-sized waterproof chest for my camera and a few other supplies. Andy also picked out some sleeping gear, while I bought some spare paddles. I figured if my canoe turned out to be not entirely seaworthy, my paddles should be; so I picked out sturdy but lightweight and extremely buoyant paddles. I made sure I had a good selection of charts and a waterproof logbook to record my travels and things I would see and experience.

Finally, we got a five-gallon container to hold my fresh water and also to serve as ballast in the bow of the canoe. Andy surprised me by paying for all of it himself.

It was Monday, August 17, 1970, when we stowed my new gear in his station wagon with the canoe tied down on top and headed east toward New York. Along the way, I pulled out my new maps and talked with Andy about my route, which would be quite easy to follow, because all I had to do was keep land on my starboard (right) side at all times. I took my blue pen and marked the route going around the Gulf of Mexico past Texas to Mexico, then to Central America, and from there to the Panama Canal and up north along the coast of the Pacific Ocean to Los Angeles, California.

- Meet the press -

I settled on Sandy Hook Bay, New Jersey, for my first stop. It was a prominent, easy-to-access landmark. After a few hours we arrived at our destination: Great Kills Yacht Basin on Staten Island, New York. Andy got out of the car, but I sat looking out across Lower Bay. Andy walked over to a throng of people, clearly speaking to them as he pointed back at me. Some of them had cameras, others had microphones from TV and radio stations, and still others merely had notebooks. Amid the reporters I recognized some friends from Allentown. Andy must have made a lot of calls. I opened the door and stepped out toward them. The press interviewed me eagerly, asking about my route, my equipment, and my motivation for the trip.

My motivation? I didn't really know what I was trying to prove. I was an alcoholic Army vet divorced from the love of my life, unemployed, and homeless. I was totally unmoored, so I didn't need to inform a soul of my plans. Hell, LA was as good a destination as any, and making the trip in a canoe would at least be some sort of accomplishment in my lackluster life. I tried to answer all their questions the best I could, but the entire time I was uncomfortable because I was receiving so much attention.

Meanwhile, Andy busied himself with the canoe and the equipment, getting everything sorted out. A few of our Allentown friends helped him drag it to the water's edge. Finally I managed to pull away from the microphones and flashbulbs, and my friends sent me off with many good wishes. I felt a lot of support from these good people, almost as if they were getting into my canoe with me.

Andy grinned from ear to ear as I made my way down the beach to him. When I got there, I was amused to discover he and one of our friends had painted a name on the bow of the little wood-and-canvas craft: *P.S. Enterprise.* "P.S.," he explained to the press, "is for Perkin Sprandel. I'm with him in spirit even if I can't cram into the canoe!" I liked the name, and told Andy it had a nice ring to it. Finally, Andy reached into his pocket and handed me his last offering: a single, thin dime.

"Don't lose this," he told me. "It's the only cash you're getting, and it's to call me when you give up. Guess I'll talk to you in two days." He winked, and I laughed.

"After all of this? Fat chance!"

Chapter 3: **One-man Show?**

I woke up at about 4 a.m. the next day without an alarm clock. When I opened my eyes and remembered where I was, the pleasant aroma of freshly brewed coffee greeted my awakening senses. I found my new fisherman friend by a small fire, cooking up some breakfast. His thermos sat nearby. He picked up the metal cylinder with an oven mitt and offered me a cup of its contents. It was clear he'd brewed the coffee right in the thermos. I accepted gratefully, and then ate some breakfast.

"So, what's next for you?" my outdoor host asked. He removed some meat and cheese from a small ice chest to make me a sandwich to take along for my lunch.

After I finished eating my unexpected breakfast, I produced my maps, showing him the route I'd marked in the car the previous day with Andy. "Manasquan Inlet," I answered, pointing it out. "That's thirty to thirty-five miles from here, right?"

"Not a bad choice," he told me. "The entrance to the Atlantic Intracoastal Waterway—that's a good landmark. Although you may be the first solo canoeist to use it."

I gave him a look of contentment and sipped my coffee. I liked the fact I was eating fresh food, or at least not Meals-Ready-to-Eat food. I didn't have terribly good memories associated with MREs. But I supposed I'd better get used to the sea rations. I had a long trip ahead of me, after all. I had gone only a few miles on my first day, but I had made my goal of getting to Sandy Hook.

"Be careful of the tide," the fisherman continued. "It's heading out in a bit, so you'll want to paddle with it. Don't go out too far or you're liable to get carried a lot farther than would be advisable in a canoe. Keep the land in sight on your starboard side. Because you are so shallow in the water, I think you'll have more problems with the winds than the current. Just remember that."

I nodded, acknowledging what he was saying, and continued to listen. He gave me tips on monitoring the tide while I traveled, how to gauge when to head back toward shore, and when to set out again. I thanked the kind man several times and accepted the lunch sandwich gladly.

Before long I was paddling out to sea. Gazing out to the horizon, I enjoyed a breathtaking view of the Atlantic Ocean. The foamy peaks of the waves dazzled like diamonds in the morning sun as they crested on the beach. The bright, new sky was clear and boasted a few large, fluffy clouds. It was definitely a pleasant change from the previous day, and my spirits were as buoyant as my canoe.

I made pretty good time with only a few obstacles to avoid. I gave a lot of consideration to what the fishermen I'd met taught me when I told them of my decision to continue this journey alone. It was clear I didn't have a great deal of experience in navigating or reading tides. And a part of me was secretly dreading the next storm or mishap to cross my path—I wouldn't admit this to anybody, of course.

On the other hand, I hadn't turned down a dare or challenge before, and I wasn't going to this time, either. I had made it through yesterday's storm, hadn't I? I had plenty of practice canoeing at camp, and enough supplies along to see me through. Manasquan Inlet was closer with every stroke of my paddle, and I was planning to use the dime Andy had given me to call him when I arrived—not to tell him I was quitting but to tell him I was continuing on the trip. He'd be glad to know the *Enterprise* was making such good time.

I was determined to do this alone. The prevailing current along the coast was favoring me. I was applying what I'd learned from the fishermen as much as I could. I couldn't help being encouraged by my progress. However, I'd been going since the early morning, and with the afternoon sun high overhead I decided to take a short rest on shore before continuing on to my next planned destination.

I paddled my way toward the long beige strip of beach less than a quarter mile distant. As I maneuvered the canoe, an unexpected surge came from beneath the boat. The surf was getting heavier and the waves stronger. One moment the water had seemed so quiet; the next I was fighting to stay afloat. Surrounded by whitecaps and quick-moving waves, I had to think and act fast.

I tried to slow myself down by paddling backward using quick, shallow strokes, but it became clear in pretty short order I wasn't abating my momentum at all. The more I fought, the more I struggled. I was tiring myself out.

"Well, if I can't fight you, I'm going to ride you to shore," I declared to the waves, reversing my paddle and pushing my little canoe and myself to the crest of the next wave. I recalled the fishermen telling me to move with the current, not against it. As the first wave dropped and I pushed myself to the next one in an exhilarating pattern, I let out a cheer because I enjoyed the fun ride.

Soon the shore was close enough to touch. With one more push of the paddle, I swept onto the sand like an expert. I stopped, still seated in the canoe, and looked around; proud of the fact I had come to a safe halt on the beach.

- Crashed down on my triumph -

I reinforced my self-confidence by quietly reassuring myself I had made it. Then I raised my arms and yelled out loud to the waves, "I made it!"

That's when the huge wave behind the little wave I'd ridden to shore crashed down on my triumph. The water grabbed the stern, lifted the canoe high into the air as if it were a child's toy boat, and flipped it over—with me still inside. For one terrifying moment I was completely under water, and since I'd been whooping and hollering like an idiot, I got a mouthful of abrasive, acrid seawater. The second my head broke the surface, I coughed and spat the stuff out, shaking my head to clear it. I was soaked to the skin and felt like a blithering fool. I took hold of the *Enterprise* and dragged her up to the beach, giving the waves a withering glare for good measure.

To my surprise, when I looked back I didn't see anything floating in the tidewaters. I flipped the canoe back over to find everything intact. I was incredibly glad I had taken the time to strap everything in.

Of course, the contents of my vessel had been jostled around from the capsizing, since the contents had not been tied tightly. So instead of enjoying some cold brews like I'd planned to do, I spent several hours in the bright afternoon sun untying and rearranging all the equipment and my few belongings to allow them to dry out. The flies on the beach seemed to be picking the salt from the seawater out of my hair.

Now I had to wait beside my canoe and look for an opportune moment to re-launch, lest I do a repeat performance. When the surf finally calmed after a long while, I gathered my drying items into the canoe and pushed back out to sea again.

- Manasquan Inlet -

The light faded sooner than I'd expected. Before the sun sank completely behind the waves, I checked my charts. I was running close to the shore, close to Sea Grit Lighthouse. A little farther ahead I could see the marker lights to Manasquan Inlet, and then, a little beyond them, the welcome sight of the Sea Grit's light flickering and flashing. I was safe from the ocean now, in the Intracoastal Waterway. Despite my earlier, foolish mishap, I'd stayed on the course I'd laid out.

I paddled to a dock a short distance past the lighthouse and tied up my canoe. As I was pulling myself out of it, a group of people cautiously approached the dock. They soon picked up speed, and I heard at least one person yell, "That's him!"

"Hey, aren't you Fritz?" another one of them asked.

"Yeah, that's him," a man in the back said. "I saw him on the TV last night."

Before long they started offering me food, drinks, and ice for my cooler. One of the guys had brought out a portable grill, and his wife greeted me warmly while offering me my pick of several tasty-looking fish. A few of them were also fishermen, and one of them offered me a small jar of bait. He was curious and asked if I was fishing for my food out on the ocean.

"No," I told him, "because my sponsor didn't buy me a fishing pole. I've got a case full of MREs, though."

The man frying the fish laughed. "I used to be in the service myself, Fritz. Just be careful of the cheese in those things, and take a break from 'em for a bit. Here, your fish is ready."

I gratefully took the plate he offered me. I reached down into the canoe and opened the cooler where I'd been keeping my beer. They immediately stopped me and told me that was a no-no. They told me to save my supply, and then they gave me all the beer I needed. I cracked one of theirs open and took a long drink, talking about my adventures over the last couple days with those gathered around, and how much I was looking forward to my next big stop, Atlantic City. Eventually, some of them started to head home.

"You want to stay at our place?" asked the wife of the man who'd made me dinner. "We've got a spare room, and we're just a quick walk up the pier."

"No thanks," I said. "I really appreciate the meal and everybody coming out to meet me, but I have to do this trip alone."

The woman looked at her husband and said, "We understand, Fritz, but don't worry. Something tells me you're going to keep getting help. Even if you're not looking for it." She winked and put an arm around her husband. They said their good-byes and headed for home.

- Meeting Julie -

One person stayed behind. She was young and pretty, most likely in her early twenties, and had asked me several questions about my trip while everyone had been around. I gave her a smile and then looked for somewhere to put the empty can.

"Oh, I'll take that," she said. "I can toss it in my knapsack and drop it in the garbage when I get home."

"Thank you," was my natural response to her. I was being polite, thinking we were about to part ways, but she still showed no sign of being in a hurry to end our conversation. "What's on your mind?" I finally asked, trying to determine where this extended interchange was headed.

She shrugged and looked a little shy, brushing a lock of long, black hair out of her vibrant eyes. "I just want to know more about you. Are you married?"

Thoughts of CJ and our divorce must have registered on my face. Her happy face turned to a frown, and she looked away. "I'm sorry. Forget I asked," she said apologetically as she turned to leave.

I stood up. "No… I'm the one who's sorry," I insisted. "Please, stay. Let's talk. What's your name?"

She smiled brightly. "I'm Julie."

We walked along the shore and talked for a long time. I told her the whole story, from my days in the service to my romancing CJ and the accident and the drinking that lead to our split—and all the while, Julie listened closely. She took my hand and watched my face when I told her about my struggle with alcohol. Eventually she stopped strolling and leaned over to kiss my cheek.

"Do you want to come back to my house with me?" she asked.

I knew I had to start early, though her eyes were earnest and her hand was resting on my chest.

Wow, decisions, decisions! I silently screamed to myself. I thought about it for a moment: self-indulgence or self-discipline?

"Uh, how about if you walk me back to my canoe? I have to leave early in the morning, before it's light, and I want to head out first thing. But I'll give you Andy's phone number so you can call him in the morning. You can tell him I'm not quitting, and I'm still going alone. In return, he should let you know when I finally drop my dime to call him."

She looked disappointed, but slowly nodded in agreement. We walked back to the dock hand in hand, and while we were looking over the water she gave me another kiss, a serious one on the lips this time, and didn't stop for a while. It was hard for me to finally tell her to go. I went back to the *Enterprise* and made myself as comfortable as I could in my sleeping bag, although the ribs of the canoe weren't the most ideal mattress. I was lying in the canoe thinking, *Ribs-Julie, Julie-ribs—there's something wrong with this picture.* But when at last I slept, it was alone in my sleeping bag, my canoe and me.

Chapter 4: **The Joys of Sponsorship**

The next morning cold droplets of rain on my face woke me up. I moved my arms to unzip my sleeping bag and suddenly felt a thousand protests of pain. For a moment I imagined someone had grabbed me by the wrists with both hands and twisted hard, or else I'd been in a fight and couldn't remember.

I struggled out of my sleeping bag and knelt to roll it up. I was so sore I couldn't accomplish even this simple task. I rubbed my aching muscles and did a few simple exercises, trying to keep in mind this was something I'd have to get used to. It wasn't as if anybody else were going to do the paddling for me. I wasn't about to stick an engine on a canoe—not that I could buy one with a dime. Besides, it'd be cheating.

The rain and early morning fog made it difficult to make out the flashing beacon of the lighthouse, about a half a mile distant. Convincing myself this fog was nothing compared to the soup I'd managed to survive my first day out, and bracing myself against the pain, I forced myself to settle into the *Enterprise* and cast off.

Canoeing in the Intracoastal Waterway is a lot safer than on the Atlantic Ocean, but more confusing. Going the way the crow flies—paddling in a straight line—seemed harder as I maneuvered across the bays. Manasquan Inlet, New Jersey, is only the beginning of the Intracoastal Waterway. The entire eastern Waterway is almost three thousand miles long, from its unofficial northern origin in New Jersey, heading all the way south along the Atlantic coast, wrapping around the southern tip of Florida and snaking first north, and then west and south along the Gulf of Mexico coast. The southern terminus of the Waterway is in Brownsville, Texas.

After consulting my maps, I figured I'd have to be careful not to come too close to the commercial sections of the Waterway to avoid getting plowed under, the way I nearly had been on my first dreadful day. This is also when it first sank into my brain that this dare would not be as easy as I thought. Just finding places to stop for a rest break, to recover from a storm, to camp, or to sleep overnight, I quickly realized, would be a lot more tricky for me than it was for the pioneers and explorers of earlier years when it was all just wilderness. I hadn't taken into account that federal or state government or private individuals now owned all the land along the coastline.

The rain let up soon after I left the dock. The sunlight streamed down through the quiet clouds, painting a picture-postcard scene as I worked the soreness out of my arms with every stroke of the paddle. However, the exercise wasn't as much help for my stiff back, which silently protested of the absence of a bed to sleep on the night before. Eventually I reached under my seat for my canteen and was surprised to feel something soft wrapped in plastic. Pulling the unfamiliar object out, I found it to be a bag of sandwiches double wrapped to keep them dry. Accompanying the meal was a note from the fisherman's wife I'd met the previous night:

Julie woke me up at 3 a.m. and said she didn't want you to eat MREs today. So we made these for you. We hope you like them, and that you reach Atlantic City without too much trouble. Good luck!

I thoroughly enjoyed a few of the sandwiches and continued to paddle along the shoreline toward my destination. The memories of the people's hospitality the night before and especially the thought of Julie's eyes and smile were a powerful boost to my spirits.

- Bidding the dime good-bye -

I paddled close in to shore and disembarked not long after, dragging the *Enterprise* up onto the beach, and made my way up to the lighthouse; it had been my landmark for the last day and a half now. Outside its door was a phone booth. I fished around in my pocket for the dime. I pulled it out and examined it—the only money Andy had given me. I slid it into the phone and made the call.

"Andy Perkin," he said.

"Andy, it's Fritz!" I replied.

"Fritz? It's great to hear from you! Where are you?"

"Just south of Barnegat Lighthouse Inlet. I should be in Atlantic City in two days."

"Good. Then I'll have time to get down to meet you."

"You're coming down?"

"Of course I am! Did you really think you'd go this entire trip without seeing the guy who's sponsoring you?"

"You've got a point," I said with a laugh. We chatted for a few more minutes, until I ran out of time on the call—before I could say good-bye or he could wish me luck. I went back down the hill and walked the canoe out into the surf, then climbed inside and started paddling once more. I held off for as long as I could before I finally ate my last sandwich.

The weather was pleasant as I traveled south toward my destination. My journey the entire day was unimpeded. The sky darkened to herald the coming night, and I knew I was right in the estimate I'd given to Andy. I paddled myself closer to shore again, and kept my eyes open for an appealing dock or beach. It started to drizzle again as I pulled my canoe onto the first beach I could find, the last rays of sunlight winking out in the west.

I settled in to relax for the evening, and noted in my logbook it was the first one I was spending alone. It was peaceful. I had a few beers and some Dewar's, and munched on one of the MREs before rolling out my sleeping bag. I looked up and down the shore as pleasant images of my walk with Julie came back to soothe my mind. Then I climbed into the bag and got some much-needed sleep.

The sun's warmth the next morning gently brought me back from my slumber, and I pulled myself up. My arms were less sore than the day before. I guess my muscles must have begun acclimating to the workload. I had what I would call the "Fritz Sprandel Special" for breakfast, because it had a little more flair than "MRE." It was soup this time, but since I had no way to start a fire, I ate it cold. After a drink of fresh water, the *Enterprise* and I were on our way once more.

I continued to be surprised at the sheer number of bays, inlets and islands I discovered as I navigated along the shore. When I saw my first map of the United States, the coast seemed relatively smooth. Now I was seeing it up close and personal, and it amazed me. Drawing every one of these features would have taken a magnifying glass, a fine-tipped marker, and a skilled, steady hand.

The advantage of all the little islands around me was I could paddle toward my destination free from the Atlantic winds, the source of storms like the one I'd run into my first day; the disadvantage was I now had all sorts of currents, riptides, and undertows to deal with. But the instructions the fishermen had given me helped me make it through the narrows without a serious or dangerous incident—including another ornery wave to flip me over.

- Atlantic City by sunset -

It was mid-afternoon when I reached the Atlantic City Expressway and passed under the bridge connecting the mainland to the shore points. I could clearly hear cars and trucks rumbling along above me. The famous hotels of the city towered above me; by now the sun was turning a pinkish-orange as it started to slip behind them. People walking across the bridges stopped to watch a nut in a canvas canoe carefully making his way through a veritable fleet of luxury boats.

The dying sunlight reflecting off the hotel windows and billboards was breathtaking. I stowed my paddle and fished out my camera to snap some photos of the scenery. I finally came to an unoccupied spot on one of the piers, tied up the *Enterprise*, and climbed onto the dock.

I was surprised to see someone on the opposite end of the dock jumping up and down, waving his arms like an idiot. He was standing next to a pay phone. I walked toward him, curious. Two cars pulled up right in front of me. The doors flew open, and out popped all the friends I'd last seen in New York. The jumping jack was Andy Perkin, and he had a huge grin on his face. He gave me a hug, inadvertently triggering explosions of pain in my strained muscles. But despite the aches, it was great to see him.

"After you disappeared into that fog I wasn't sure I was ever going to see you again!" he confessed to me, slapping me on the shoulder. "I had Steve watching the bay from the hotel."

He was referring to Steve Bell, who was a manager at the Ale House in Allentown. I always told my friends that Steve was the man in charge of general riffraff and disorganization at the Ale House. He'd become my best friend not long after my motorcycle accident, mostly because I spent so much time at the Ale House.

"I suppose you got yourself a hotel room here then?" I inquired.

"We got a few," Andy replied with a big smile while guiding me to the car. "And we got one for you, too. We figured you could use a shower before we start the party."

The mention of a party made me happy. Then one of my friends in the group asked me if I was really going to continue the trip. If he had asked me when I was alone, out on the water, the answer might have been different. However, surrounded once again by my good buddies and on dry land, I found myself responding, "Yes."

I didn't have time for the full shower I'd been craving since the first morning I'd awakened to find my muscles sore and aching. All I could manage was to stick my head under the showerhead and wash out some of the salt from my hair before the room phone rang, and I heard a familiar voice.

"Hi, Fritz!" Julie said. "Come on down—you're the guest of honor!" I didn't have to be asked twice.

I walked into a huge party in full swing when I arrived downstairs at the bar. It was great to be with that old gang of mine again exchanging hugs and catching up on all the news from Allentown. Barry and Dave, good friends of Andy and me who worked at the Ale House back home, soon started comparing the Ale House to the hotel's bar. The more they drank, the more critical they got.

Andy found the whole thing quite amusing, as did Julie, who fit in well with the crowd. She told me she'd called Andy first thing the morning after I'd left her, and he'd made arrangements to pick her up on his way to Atlantic City. She and I talked more, and I felt more of a bond between us, and soon her shyness faded into familiarity and affection.

We sang some songs we knew, and I told everyone about how I made it through the storm and flipped over in the canoe. My stories caused howls of laughter, and I received a lot of compliments for surviving the ordeal. Eventually the partygoers started to get tired and drop out, and Andy, Dave, Julie, and I headed back upstairs.

We sat in Andy's room for a while and chatted, and then Julie tugged on my hand and whispered something seductive in my ear, something I did not want to repeat to anyone else. I warmed to her suggestion, and we headed for the door, but Andy told me to hold on. As I turned to Andy, Julie kissed my cheek and stepped out of the room.

"I just wanted to say… I'm glad you're all right," he said. "I really was worried when you left and headed into that fog. I didn't think you were this serious about the trip."

"Andy, I spent an hour at the Ale House that night convincing you I was serious," I reminded him. "And you of all people should know, when I take a dare, I take it seriously. It's how I crossed the country by land; I ever tell you about my winter jaunt?"

"Yeah," he replied with a nod, "a few times, in fact."

"Then I'm not going to bore you by repeating it."

When I opened the door, I found the hallway empty. Andy gently put his hand on my shoulder, telling me once more, "Fritz, just be careful. That's all I wanted to say, really, before you head out again or anything. And this girl, she's really nice, and great to look at, but…"

"Andy, I know you're my friend and I appreciate what you're saying, but I'm really not in the mood for an 'it's too soon' speech. The divorce is final, and besides, it's not like you brought CJ along, right? Hell, I don't even know where she is. So just let it go, okay?"

He looked at me sheepishly and shook his head. "I'm sorry, Fritz."

"It's okay—you're tryin' to look out for me," I responded as he nodded and finally let go of me. "Get some sleep. I'll see you in the morning."

- Shower time -

I headed down the hall to my room, and didn't see anyone when I entered. Finally, I was able to fully enjoy the shower and the sensation of hot water easing the tension in the muscles of my arms and back. My fingers moved to knead the various knots days of paddling and sleeping on uncomfortable surfaces had left behind. The feelings were so pleasant and soothing I didn't hear the door open and close. When I felt the draft on my skin, I knew I wasn't alone.

Looking over my shoulder I saw Julie joining me in the shower, wearing only her dazzling smile, with mischief glittering in her eyes.

"Hi there," was all she said at first. "Andy gave me a spare key." She saw what I'd been doing with my hands on my shoulders. "Let me do that for you," she purred, and massaged my back. It was a supremely delightful feeling because I hadn't been touched by another person for some time now. The mighty waters of the Atlantic Ocean had carried me up to this stage of my journey, but I was afloat on different waves this night, and they had a current and power all their own. I didn't get to sleep for a long time, and when I finally did, with a pretty, young woman beside me, I drifted off thinking this was the best trip ever.

Chapter 5: **The Atlantic Intracoastal Waterway**

A loud knocking on the door woke me early the next morning. Julie was passed out cold. I rolled out of bed and opened the door to find reporters outside. I was starting to get used to the unpleasant intrusion of tape recorders and microphones shoved in my face, and I gave the photographers a friendly smile as I emerged, closing the door behind me. I didn't want them to wake Julie, but I also didn't want to leave their questions unanswered.

They asked me about my experiences so far and my planned route. I responded with the stories of the storm, the fishermen, and fighting the waves. Andy arrived while I was still talking to the reporters, looking on approvingly with a cup of coffee in his hand. It smelled fantastic, and I gave him a glance as the reporters thanked me for talking to them. When they dispersed, Andy walked over.

"Mind if I buy you breakfast?" he asked me.

"Might be the last hot meal I have in a while, so no, I wouldn't mind at all!" I replied with a grin, and we headed downstairs for coffee, eggs, bacon, and toast. After a few bites, Andy looked me straight in the eye.

"What did you mean by that crack about a hot meal?"

"Well, I'm going back out there today, and I can't exactly cook up hot food in a canvas canoe," I explained.

He paused. "You know, Fritz, I honestly didn't think you'd make it this far. It's not that I don't believe in you, it's because the ocean isn't something you really want to play with, especially in a canoe."

I smiled and shrugged, trying to explain. "Andy, it hasn't been easy, by any stretch. But I'm having a great time. I'm really glad I decided to do this, and there's no way I'm going to quit."

"You've got great resolve," Andy responded, "but I know you're aware how bad it can get out in the open water. I heard your story about the storm and how a wave nearly drowned you."

"All the wave did was humble me a bit," I told him while I sipped my coffee. "I'm definitely going to be more careful in the future, but now, since I've started, I want to see this through to the end. I might feel differently when I'm alone out on the water, but I know there'll always be a shore waiting for me. It'll be difficult, but I know it will all be worth it in the end."

"I really don't want you to get hurt or worse," he moaned. "It really is rough out at sea. You know, more than once I've wondered if I did the right thing supplying this trip and letting you go out in the elements alone. I'm your friend; I wouldn't be a very good one if I didn't worry."

I gave my friend an understanding smile. "I really do appreciate your concern, Andy. But remember I'm not doing this only for myself. Any time somebody sees me or my little canoe, they're seeing you too.

It's not called the *P.S. Enterprise* because it's a 'post script,' after all. The P.S. stands for 'Perkin Sprandel,' because this is something we're both doing. I'm out piloting this boat for both of us. Remember this, and it might help you when I tell you I'm not quitting."

He shrugged his shoulders and nodded slowly as if to signify his reluctant agreement. We finished breakfast talking about the festivities of the night before and the next leg of my journey. Finally I made my way back upstairs to my room. I unlocked the door and opened it, fully expecting Julie to be waiting for me in the bed.

- A handwritten note -

Unfortunately the only thing on the bed other than the sheets was a handwritten note.

"Dear Fritz," it read, "I'm sorry I couldn't wait around to say good-bye when you cast off, but I have a few things to take care of back home. But once I have them squared away, I'm driving down toward my mom's place in Florida. I'm going to call Andy every day to check on your progress, and of course I'll be looking for you on TV and in the papers.

"You're a fantastic man, Fritz. I know you've been through a lot and sometimes you feel like you've lost your direction. But I think you're finding it. What you're doing is brave and exciting, and you deserve nothing but the highest praise for it. I hope to see you again soon, even if I have to drive to California to meet you in Los Angeles.

"Love, Julie."

While I was disappointed I didn't get to say good-bye in person, I couldn't deny the warmth and joy I felt as I tenderly folded up her note and tucked it away in my pocket. At the front desk of the hotel, I asked for a small plastic bag, and luckily for me the clerk had one.

I placed the note in the bag and used clear tape to seal it shut. I was hoping it wouldn't be contaminated by seawater the rest of the way to California.

I called up to Andy's room from the lobby and told him I was leaving. He came down immediately and then drove me to the dock. He helped me into the *P. S. Enterprise,* handed me a fresh dime, then shook my hand and wished me luck one last time. I cast off and pushed away from the dock with my paddle. Then I checked the sun's position and made my way back out into the Intracoastal Waterway. It was a quiet morning, with a few clouds and bright sunshine, and I once again found myself lost in the sights and sounds of Atlantic City, watching its visitors and inhabitants bustling along their busy ways.

- The powerboat -

Suddenly, a boat's whistle caught my attention. I looked up from the school of fish I saw swimming alongside me to discover a sightseeing powerboat. The tourists called out and waved. They'd probably paid for tickets to see whales or dolphins, and probably hadn't expected to see some crazy guy in a canoe. I waved back and grinned. I was starting to get used to the idea of being a celebrity.

I paddled slowly and let the boat drift by. That is, I thought it was drifting by. As it moved past me, however, it began to dawn on me that this vessel was still moving under power, lots of power—in fact, more than enough power to slap the *Enterprise* around like a kid splashing his favorite plastic boat around in the bathtub.

I soon had to paddle hard just to stay upright. I shifted my weight and paddled against the powerboat's wake. Whatever I was doing, however, wasn't right. My canoe began taking on water. I tried paddling the other way, but it seemed to make the situation much worse. Before

I knew it, I was sitting in water up to my ankles while I paddled fiercely.

As the boat moved on, its wake spread, and although it soon dispersed, I was still fighting almost as hard to stay on course and upright. I was yelling now, and every splash of water in my face made me scream louder and grow angrier. After what seemed like an hour, I felt the *Enterprise* grind into the shoreline. I immediately hopped out, still yelling and screaming and cursing, and dragged my little craft onto the shore to dry her out. I grabbed my gear and slapped down a camp without much thought—other than how angry I was. It was the end of another day.

The warm morning sun woke me the next day. It was as bright as the day before, and the clear, calm sky was a boost to my somewhat downtrodden spirit. I gathered up my things and found the *Enterprise* dried out and ready for another few miles in the open ocean.

I put out to sea thinking the Intracoastal Waterway was probably full of powerboats like the one I'd encountered the day before, including in the non-commercial lanes, and I would have to be mindful of their mighty engines from now on if I wanted to avoid another soaking. I compared my experience to the things the fishermen had taught me and slowly discovered I was paddling with a lot more effort than I had before.

- New Jersey to Delaware in eighteen hours -

The waves of the open ocean were stronger than I could've imagined. As tired as I'd gotten during the last few days, I knew I'd be in more terrible shape after this day. I didn't really know what was in store, however, until I committed myself to crossing the massive Delaware River Bay. It's seventeen miles across the bay, plus the five miles I had already paddled north of North Cape May to take advantage the river's current, knowing it could carry me out in the Atlantic Ocean if I didn't start from a position further north.

Eighteen hours after making the decision to cross, my arms were making promises of a week's worth of pain to come. I was only a short distance from my planned destination, ending up instead at Cape Henlopen.

Despite the throbbing soreness in my muscles, I was proud of the job I was doing riding these waves. Unlike riding the powerboat's wake the day before, I was paddling through these swells like a champ. Wave after wave, I remembered what I'd learned so far on my travels, and I kept myself on course, the water out of the canoe, and, therefore, myself dry inside the canoe. The *Enterprise* might well have had sails and been carried by a levanter, as graceful and fast as she was heading for the shore. The last wave pulled my boat and me onto the beach, and I felt a real sense of accomplishment.

I pulled myself out of the boat and tried to step away from the water. But like my arms, my legs were sore and weakened—in fact, so weakened they couldn't hold my weight. My ankles buckled, and I fell to my hands and knees. I was still smiling, though. I'd made it to the beach after yesterday's humiliation, and I was convinced I now had this whole ocean navigation bit nailed down. I lay down on the beach, pulled out one of my maps, and spread it out to plan my next move.

- End-over-end -

That's when the next wave hit the shore. And it hit with such force that it picked up the *Enterprise* and flipped it end-over-end. It crested high through the air and crashed loudly into the beach. My ice chest slid to a stop against my leg and my provisions flew every which way.

I spewed out a vile curse, angry at the waves and indeed angrier at my own arrogance and stupidity. I pushed myself up, turned her back over and threw everything back in. Not bothering to strap them down, I climbed back in and pushed off from the beach, setting back out for my original destination, four miles away.

Four tries later, my entire body now screaming at me in protest, and the *Enterprise* half-filled with water, I finally made it through those waves. I clambered out and dragged my boat up as far from the water as I could. I pulled my sleeping bag free and basically rolled over on the sand until it was wrapped around me, and then dropped to sleep from pure exhaustion.

Chapter 6: **Alone in the Marshes**

When I awoke the next day, I decided I was going take the Lewis and Rehoboth canal as much as possible and try to avoid the major shipping lanes. I checked my map and marked a couple of areas I judged more likely to contain landmarks easy to pick out from the coast. Satisfied I'd come up with a workable plan instead of haphazardly winging it, I gathered my gear into the *Enterprise* and set off southward. Every hour or two I consulted my route and found I had done well choosing landmarks.

However, I was still in the Intracoastal Waterway. These were routes dense with vegetation, traversed only by small boats with motors. Now I'd heard of large, flat-bottomed boats with huge fans on the back that could literally propel them on top of the water. I was not so fortunate, however, and took my time paddling through the long, lonely slopes of those wet moors.

- The long, lonely slopes of the wet moors -

Days went by. I secured my canoe to whatever I could find during the night and slept on the spot. I learned the marshlands could be deceptive. Once I felt I had found a patch of ground to sleep on for a change, and tried to step out of my canoe. Unfortunately, my foot went right through a carpet of moss, and I sank down to my knee in dirty water—I almost fell out of the *Enterprise,* which would have rolled her over on top of me. Thankfully, I had kept my hands firmly clasped onto the boat and was able to pull myself back up without capsizing.

The more time I spent in the moors, the more I started to analyze and re-think the route I'd picked out the last time I'd slept on a beach. I tried to determine if I could have known in advance my course would have taken me into this labyrinth. It took me the better part of a day to convince myself I'd done nothing wrong when I charted my course. I was losing precious time—it'd been almost a week, by now, since I'd seen the ocean. Looking around all I saw was swamp, swamp, and more swamp.

After a while, my nose had grown accustomed to the loamy odor, or maybe I was starting to smell a heck of a lot like the marshlands around me. Either way, I was becoming increasingly concerned about finding a way out. More than once I spotted my destination in the distance and tried to find a path in front of me toward it. However the swamp had an annoying habit of sloping down toward a copse of trees or a tangle of underwater ferns and growth nasty enough to hinder and turn my little canoe.

I ran into one dead end after another, and it seemed like my journey might end in those marshes. The mosquitoes were the loudest and biggest things I ever saw. And worst of all, I was running low on beer.

Finally, a couple of days after losing sight of the ocean, I had to conclude the only way I was going to get back out to sea was if I sought help. But I had no idea where to go to find another person. I was uncertain as to my exact location and had no idea how far I'd come into the swamp. The only thing I knew for sure, as the sun went down at the close of another day: I was hopelessly lost, and all I had accomplished with my aimless paddling was to get myself into more trouble.

- Tied to a buoy -

I was nearly exhausted. I wanted to conserve my provisions (including the beer and Dewar's), so I glided toward the only man-made light in sight. It sat atop a small, rusty buoy, swaying gently in the breeze. It was a dull red color, pocked with brown spots of rust and an occasional smear of bird droppings; but to me it was a thing of beauty—it was the first sign of human life I'd seen all in a long time. I figured someone had to pass by this spot eventually. So I tied the *Enterprise* to the buoy and decided to lie back and look at the stars.

Nighttime in a swamp is awesome. The lack of artificial light makes the tiniest stars peek out of the blackness of the night sky and twinkle like little diamonds. The sky is full of stars, not something you usually see in a city, not even in a medium-size city like Allentown. And the noises—crickets, frogs, buzzing insects, mosquitoes, and the soft, wet sounds of snakes and other critters gliding through the water—combine in a sort of natural symphony to underscore the marsh's rugged, natural beauty. The whole place has a peace about it, though it's quite different from being at sea.

I didn't notice I had fallen asleep until I felt a calloused hand on my shoulder, gently shaking me awake. A voice near my head with a slight drawl was saying, "Hey. Hey, buddy, wake up."

I blinked my eyes, and my vision focused on a man wearing a wide-brimmed straw hat, his jaw line hidden by an unkempt beard. In his other hand he was holding a fishing rod. He was eye-level with me when I sat up, meaning he too was sitting. His aluminum canoe was right beside the wood-and-canvas hull of the *Enterprise*, and an outboard motor sat ready behind him.

"You okay, friend?" he gently asked me as he looked me over, one eyebrow raised. "You look like you've had quite a journey."

"I have," I replied, looking up at the sky and the shimmering rays of sunlight now piercing the clouds. It was early morning by my reckoning. I rubbed the sleep from my eyes and moved to untie myself from the buoy, telling him of my journey.

"Want to restock that ice chest of yours, brother?" He was smiling broadly at me, clearly intrigued by the recounting of my travels up to that point. "Trip like that must make a man mighty thirsty."

"That it does," I confirmed with a vigorous nod. "I was just thinking of having a drink and maybe something to eat. Canned beans," I continued, picking up one of the cans and showing it to the fisherman, "the breakfast of champions."

"Aw, save those for some other time," he told me, patting my shoulder. "My name's Joe. Follow me to the port and I'll fix you up."

Joe obliged me by refraining from using his motor. We paddled together to a pier not far from the buoy I had found the night before. Tied to the opposite side of the pier where we secured our canoes were three other boats with men onboard, each one tending to catches or getting ready for a day's fishing. I could smell eggs and grits, and Joe invited me to have some breakfast. I thanked him, and happily joined him and his friends, catching the others up on how I'd happened to travel into the swampland. We talked until the coffee and eggs were all gone.

Soon some of the other men at their pier decided they could spare some time off and brought a few cans of beer on board, then began asking me about Atlantic City, the boats I'd seen, and the sort of route I had planned out.

Finally, after what seemed like only a couple of hours, I looked over to the *Enterprise* and resolved to get out of this swamp, as pleasant as the company was.

"Thanks again for the grits," I said to Joe, "and for the conversation." I nodded around the boat to the others. "Looks like I'm about ready to be on my way."

"You really want to paddle out against the tide right now?" Joe asked in response, looking up at the dying sunlight. I must have lost track of time while Joe and his friends had taken care of me. By now the sun was beginning to sink behind the low, curved mounds of earth lying partly submerged beneath the murky waters usually plied by large fish and mean, hungry crabs.

"No… I guess that wouldn't be very smart," I finally replied to my newfound friends, flashing them my pearly whites. They grinned in response, but more to one another than to me. "Did I say something funny?" I asked, feeling a bit confused.

"Want something to *really* clear your cobwebs?" Joe asked with a wink. "It's a bit of a secret, mind you, so you can't tell folks about it. We're in a dry county, after all, so this isn't exactly what one'd call legal." His friends were nodding to one another, and I saw one whispering to the other. My eyes narrowed. Joe looked over his shoulder at them, and then winked. "Ah, no big deal, Fritz, they're just makin' sure they're all right with you tagging along."

- Drinking moonshine and swapping stories -

"We sure are," said one of them. "We want to hear more of his stories, especially if that Julie chickadee is involved!" They chuckled a bit among themselves, nudging one another the way guys do. I felt a bit embarrassed about the waterproofed note I carried in my pocket, but I put thoughts of Julie out of my mind for now. I wasn't exactly sure where the evening was going from here, but I'd set out looking for adventure, and this certainly fit the bill, albeit completely unexpectedly.

One of Joe's friends had a rather beat-up looking Oldsmobile, and we piled in. He drove down a dirt road to a small, rural street unmarked by signs or stripes. About fifteen minutes later, he took another turn, and the rough ride told me the road, if it could indeed be called a road, was not only unpaved, but also obviously rarely traveled. We pulled up outside a long, low farmhouse, which had only a couple of lights lit inside. Our driver turned off the engine, then flicked the headlights off. He waited a moment, then flipped them back on. He repeated this process twice.

The porch light came on at the farmhouse. I wasn't sure what the blinking had been all about, and none of Joe's friends had said anything since we'd left the docks. But we piled out of the car and walked up the lawn toward the long porch. A man who looked like he belonged in the ZZ Top band awaited us in the open door, stroking his long, frazzled beard.

Joe patted my arm when we approached the fuzzy doorkeeper. "Zeke, this here is Fritz, and he's canoein' from New York to LA by way of the open ocean!"

"I read about this cat in the paper," Zeke responded, taking my hand. "Not every night we get a celebrity in here. C'mon in, Fritz."

I was led to the back of the house and into a large room with huge metal vents on the walls concealing industrial-sized fans. "I have to keep the room ventilated," Zeke told me, "so this don't blow up in my face. Joe and his pals bring in yeast and all the other ingredients, and we put it all in this here still."

He patted a metal contraption that looked like it had been cobbled together from spare parts. I couldn't name every component, but I saw two oilcans, a large metal drum, and what appeared to be a car radiator. Zeke put a metal pitcher under a spigot and gently pulled a lever to dispense some clear liquid; it smelled a bit like turpentine. "It don't smell too pretty, but after a couple sips you might not be feelin' your nose anyhow."

Joe patted my shoulder again. "Here you go, Fritz. This'll save your beer and whiskey rations. Have a bit of Zeke's moonshine."

I took the metal mug he offered me and held my nose for the first sip. It burned going down my throat, but I immediately felt its effects. I followed Zeke, Joe, and the others back outside, where we sat on the porch and listened to the noises of the woods around us.

"So I think you owe me at least one story 'bout how you came to be here," Zeke told me, taking a drink from his own mug. I agreed with him, and began once again to recount my travels.

Chapter 7: **Chesapeake Companion**

I could not remember a time when my head pounded as mercilessly as it did the next morning. I yearned for a cup of fresh, strong coffee but wondered if it would do me any good as I paddled along, having left the marshes and the moonshine far behind me. Joe and Zeke had ridden with me back down to the docks, and Joe had towed me out toward the ocean and wished me luck, handing me a small Mason jar with a bit of clear liquid I knew was Zeke's hooch. My head felt like John Henry was working on a railroad in my brain.

I eased the *Enterprise* out into the open water, and leaned back a bit, dipping into the cooler to search for the Mason jar. I figured maybe some "hair of the dog" would help me recover enough to navigate. I opened the jar's lid, had a tiny sip, and felt a jolt throughout my system. I almost barfed over the side of the canoe, but my headache lessened.

I replaced the jar and switched to beer, sipping it and letting the waves buffet the canoe a little. The movement was actually rather soothing, and it did wonders for my head. I laid my paddle across my knees and closed my eyes, enjoying the taste of the beer and the sound of the waves.

I grew hungry and decided to fix myself an MRE. It certainly wasn't my first choice for a meal, but I had eaten most of my fresh food and wanted to conserve what I had left. Still, I couldn't deny it was sitting pretty heavily in my stomach as I continued paddling. I did the same thing for supper in the evening, and breakfast the next morning. Before long, I came within sight of my next landmark, and a navigational guide to boot: the Chesapeake Bay Bridge-Tunnel.

- Crossing the Chesapeake Bay -

The bridge was truly a marvel to behold. I'd driven over it before, but to see it from below was a whole new experience. I paddled along gently, enjoying from a new perspective the engineering behind the huge pylons put together to hold up the tons of concrete and pavement now enabling people to commute freely across the bay on a dry road. I made my strokes slow, wondering if any of the travelers on the bridge could see me down below street level.

They didn't at first. But at the point where the bridge begins to slope down toward the tunnel, I saw people in their cars and vans pointing and waving, so I acknowledged their greetings and waved back. The kids especially seemed curious why some loony with a slightly bushy beard and reddened skin was paddling his way across the bay in a dinky wood-and-canvas canoe.

They weren't the only ones to notice me, either. As I made my way across the bay, a large cargo ship blew its horn. The deck crew was waving and calling out to me. I raised my paddle and heard a cheer. It was a markedly different experience from the first time I'd heard a horn so close by on my first harrowing day in the fog. Despite all the attention from my friends, this was the first time I'd received so much public attention. I was well into my journey, and I'd be lying if I said it didn't make me feel good.

I indulged myself with one of the few remaining apples I'd been saving. The fruit was juicy, sweet, and tasty, a welcome change from an MRE. I also downed a sip of moonshine, followed by a healthy dose of fresh water.

The last thing I needed was to dehydrate myself on the open ocean. As I looked about, it seemed like my crossing of the mighty Chesapeake Bay was going to pass without major incident. I was moving along the other side of the bridge, paddling slowly and steadily. I had to conserve my strength. I still had plenty of bay to cross, and I didn't want to wear myself out before I reached solid ground.

- The shark -

Then I heard something stir in the water on the starboard side of the *Enterprise*. I looked toward the ripples and saw a gray fin slip up out of the water. It was close enough for me to reach out and touch. I leaned over, curious to see if a dolphin had taken an interest in me. However, as its massive head rose a bit from the water, made a run toward my boat, and bumped into it, I suddenly recognized the huge, gray creature swimming beside me—it was not a porpoise, but a shark!

I suddenly felt exposed and vulnerable in my little conveyance of wood and canvas, something all too easy for a shark's teeth to tear through. Now I'd heard stories of people being chased or caught and bitten by sharks who'd survived by punching the predator in the nose. So, ready with my left hook, I kept on paddling, and with a heck of a lot more urgency. The shark took another couple rushes at my canoe. But soon it seemed to grow bored and inexplicably swam away.

I soon came to my senses, now that the danger had passed, and discovered I'd been holding my breath the whole time since I first identified the shark; so I exhaled and relaxed, reaching into my cooler for a beer. If I had to pick a time during my crossing of the bay when I felt truly justified in drinking, this incident would have been it.

The next few days were rather uneventful and, thankfully, shark-free. I was back to my usual diet of MREs and beer. It was difficult for me to ration the alcohol. Every time I cracked open a new can I reminisced about the Ale House back in Allentown and the number of times I woke up outside with nowhere to go except back inside, and nothing to do but order another. But then I remembered my friends as they'd seen me off and the things I'd seen and experienced already. I recalled Julie's pretty face and the way the sunrise had illuminated the open ocean.

While paddling into a similar sunrise on the fourth day in the bay area, watching the sky slowly change from black into midnight blue to slowly reveal clouds tinged with pink by the returning sun, I first caught sight of the massive U.S. Navy warships moored like slumbering titans outside Norfolk, Virginia.

Coming into the harbor, I felt as if I had magically morphed into a live IMAX movie filming in Hampton Roads. I blinked my eyes several times as I gazed around at the landscape. I say, "landscape" rather than "seascape" because the gray hulls of the warships were like huge cliffs rising up all around me. It was no wonder the United States is renowned for commanding the mightiest fleet in the world. The morning light reflected off the portholes and bridges of the mammoth warships, silent sentinels guarding our shoreline.

LHEBERLING '09

    I felt like a tiny matchstick drifting through a forest of redwoods. The variation in boat sizes was huge, from the tiniest patrol boat to the gargantuan battleship. I got an eyeful of almost every kind of ship in the fleet with the notable exception of an aircraft carrier. But it was okay by me; it was one less warship to accidentally run me over the way an eighteen-wheeler can roll over a mouse. I took my time paddling through the bay to enjoy all the sights, and then continued on my way south.

- *The Dismal Swamp* -

In the afternoon, I consulted my maps over yet another MRE. Up ahead was the Dismal Swamp Canal. I wasn't sure if the Army Corps of Engineers was about to let my little wood-and-canvas vessel through the mighty gates, but the alternative was to cut through the Dismal Swamp itself. I didn't exactly relish the idea of paddling through more marshland, but I knew for sure going that way would allow me to keep my own pace and not compete or tangle with any larger vessels. So, after a night ashore in my sleeping bag, I cut the *Enterprise* along the shoreline until I reached the swamps.

As I navigated the narrows of this new marshland, I recalled reading about somebody who had proposed plans to turn a swamp in Virginia into a wildlife preserve. I wasn't sure if this was the one. I did, however, take pains not to disturb any of the flora or fauna more than I had to with my passage—not that I had been carelessly tossing beer cans over the side of the *Enterprise* to begin with—but here I was especially careful.

I was reminded more than once of the swamp where I'd met Joe and Zeke and their friends. I had my last bit of moonshine to commemorate them, and found out my previous experience had prepared me for navigating through this swampland, as well as maintaining my bearings. It wasn't easy, however, given the way the navigable waterways would shrink to no more than a few feet wide. More than once I had to push my paddle against semi-solid earth to keep myself moving. This did not last long, however, and by the end of the day a vast lake seemed to appear out of nowhere.

After the occasionally claustrophobic narrows of the marshes, the acres of open water were a welcome relief. I learned later I had crossed Lake Drummond. It was pristine and relaxing, especially while the sun was beginning to sink in the west. As the light faded, I resolved to make camp on the lake's shore, and also to stock up on a few supplies, provided I could find a way to do so without depriving me of my one thin dime.

I pulled the *Enterprise* up on shore and made my way across a small gravel lot to a rather rough roadway cut through the tree line surrounding the lake. Eventually I came to a major road, and right across the road was a trailer park. I walked in and found several local residents building a campfire in the middle of a circle of mobile homes. My luck seemed to be holding, at least for now. I soon learned, however, luck had very little to do with the next turn of events.

"Your fire looks mighty inviting," I said after the fire had been lit. "Would you mind if I joined you?"

One of the locals recognized me from a sporting magazine and eagerly welcomed me to sit and relax. It turned out more than a couple of the people living near the lake had canoes of their own they took on trips all over the area, so they were naturally curious about how mine was faring at sea. I told several stories from my travels, and in the course of talking ran out of cigarettes. I asked my friend for one, and before I knew it people were handing me entire packs. I must have received four or five packs before the night was out. Their generosity was nothing short of overwhelming.

As I talked with everyone, I noticed an old man across the fire that listened with interest to everything I said but didn't ask any questions or make any comments. He simply looked at me with an odd twinkle in his eye. I didn't think much about it at night when I went to sleep, but at the time I had no idea he would be the reason both my story and my life would never be the same.

Chapter 8: **An Old Man's Gift**

Since I'd gone to sleep not far from the fire, I woke up warm and well rested. The lingering embers glowed softly nearby, and wisps of light gray smoke curled up and away into the chilly morning air. I slowly wrestled my way out of the sleeping bag and rolled it up, gathering some of my other belongings as I did. I was bundling my things together when I heard a screen door whine open and slam shut.

The old man I'd seen last night came ambling toward me across the sandy ground. He was remarkably chipper for the hour of the morning—it had to be between 5 and 6 a.m. by my reckoning. He shook my hand and introduced himself as "Paul."

"Well, nice to meet you, Paul," I told him, looking toward the path I'd followed into the trailer park, "but I probably should be on my way. If I linger too long, I'm liable to burn daylight."

"Are you sure I can't interest you in a spot of breakfast?" Paul asked me with a persuasive tone in his voice. I saw smoke from his stove wafting into the air, and it occurred to me he'd already put a lot of effort into some sort of elaborate meal for more than one person. So I agreed, picked up my things to carry with me, and followed him inside.

I wasn't expecting the surprises waiting for me in his modest-looking trailer. The first delight to strike me was the deep, rich scent of fresh-brewed coffee wafting through the room as we approached the kitchen. It was clear he had been up for at least an hour making preparations for me. I'd barely spoken three words to him the night before, and here he was getting breakfast ready for me.

- A breakfast fit for a king -

He pulled out a chair for me from under a small round table and then moved quickly to the stove, looking somewhat worried. His expression softened when he saw he hadn't overcooked the eggs or the thick, lean steak he had cooking in his skillets. He pulled out a saucepan, poured some grits into it and, continuing to cook, asked me for details about things like my shark encounter and the process of making moonshine. Finally, he turned off the stove and dished out the food onto two plates, handing me one along with a steaming mug of his aromatic coffee and a tall, cool glass of orange juice.

"I just squeezed that this morning," he said, beaming with hospitality. "I hope you don't mind taking a break from beer."

"Not at all," I replied gratefully, slicing into my steak.

As it turned out, Paul had been a canoeist as well as a kayaker himself many years ago. And like me he had served in the Army, although his experiences had been much more dangerous. He mentioned he'd been in

France and Germany, and I didn't press him for details—our breakfast was a pleasant one, and I didn't wish to darken it with war stories.

"Well," I said, pushing my plate away at last, "I think if I eat another bite, I'm going to sink my boat!"

- *"I won't tell anyone if you don't"* -

"I'm glad you ate as much as you did," my gracious host replied with a smile. We both stood up from the table, and I started to round up my things. As I was moving toward the door, I turned to thank the old man again, and found Paul standing next to me with his seemingly ever-present smile, extending his hand. I took it, and as I shook it I could feel he was putting a small, rolled piece of paper in my hand. I looked down, unrolled it, and found Andrew Jackson staring back at me. I looked at the old man and shook my head.

"Seriously," I told him, "I can make it in on my own. I've made it this far, after all."

"You're going to take this money," he replied, taking hold of my wrist with a gentle grip. He closed my hand around the bill, and then continued, "and I'm going to tell you why."

I had to admit I was curious, but I didn't pocket the twenty-dollar bill yet. I wanted to see what he had to say first. He took a seat at the table, and I sat across from him. He waited until I looked him directly in the eyes to start talking.

"Fritz, I need to tell you this. You are doing something I dearly wish I could. And I need to tell you, whether you understand it yet or not, it's really important to me—and to a lot more people than you might think—for you to carry on in your journey and do your best to reach your goals. But that's not why you should do it.

"Don't do this for anyone else in your life but yourself," he told me, the way a father tries to impart wisdom to his son. Then he explained himself wistfully. "If only I were fifty years younger, I would love to be doing what you're doing. But it's too late for me, and I never had the chance." He looked at me earnestly. "You might be living a true-life adventure story for yourself, but it's only a fantasy for me, and millions of other people like me. But although I can't go along with you, I still want to be a part of your story."

I was rooted to my chair, shocked by his words. I had been going along on my trip considering it merely another decision I'd made on the fly without giving any serious consideration to its ultimate purpose or its impact on anyone else. But now, sitting back for a while and reflecting on it with this kind gentleman, I had to admit I'd already come across many incredible experiences and people to tell about; they would all make great chapters in a story.

The old man continued, "I know you can make it on your own," he was saying, "but take the money. I won't tell anyone if you don't," he promised. And then he punctuated his final sentence with a wink. I reached across the table and took the twenty-dollar bill without another word. I was already fighting tears.

I couldn't come up with words to thank Paul. All I could do was awkwardly shake his hand again before we made our way back to the *Enterprise.* I put out to the lake, and he stood on the shore, watching me go, waving as I reached the narrow waterway leading back to the open ocean. It was mid-afternoon before I took a break to eat, and as I did, I continued to think about my morning encounter with Paul. I stretched out in the canoe and put my hands under my head.

As I lay in the *Enterprise,* letting the current rock me gently, I watched the clouds roll by high above me. Some looked tinged with shadows, carrying heavy loads of rain, while others were like tiny wisps of white painted on the roof of the world. I found myself thinking about God as well as the old man. My foot gently nudged the carton of cigarettes he'd given me, and the twenty dollars in my pocket next to my dime felt slightly heavy.

I had to conclude, no matter what I did from this point on, I had found at least one good reason for my venture. The old man wasn't going to be forgotten if I had anything to say about it. This might be my story, but he would forever be a part of it, and so would the boys who'd given me moonshine, and also lovely young Julie. None of them would be forgotten. I knew it, God knew it, and that settled it.

- Luckless mother -

A couple of days later I decided to treat myself to a small, non-MRE breakfast. It was late morning by the time I found a suitable place, but I found a marina with a diner nearby. I walked in and ordered coffee, and was settling on an omelet for breakfast when a woman came in looking tired and worn. She sat at the counter and quietly ordered a bowl of cereal. Then she started to cry. She looked so dejected I felt compelled to get up and walk over to the counter beside her to ask her what was wrong.

"I miss my daughter so much," she told me. "I've been so down on my luck ever since her father died. They fired me at work because I couldn't meet the quotas, and we got evicted from our house. I used the money I had left to send my daughter to my sister's place in Pittsburgh, and I've been trying to find a job ever since. It's slow going, but I'm doing my best to keep at it, although lately I have been discouraged by the lack of any good possibilities around here.

"I guess that's why I'm here," she concluded, stirring the cold cereal with her spoon. "I don't have much money left. In fact I'll be lucky if I can afford another bowl of cereal like this. But the way my luck has been, I have this feeling something else is going to happen." She looked up at me. "Am I a horrible mother for sending my daughter away?"

I reflected on what she had said for a moment while I sipped my coffee. I'd stopped in this diner to get something to eat, but instead I'd been guided into meeting this woman. I'd listened to her story with interest and found myself wanting to help. My talk with the old man came back to me, and I looked the woman in the eye as I shook my head.

"No, I think you did the right thing," I assured her. "But now that things have settled down a little, you really should be with her. Would your sister let you stay at her house as well?" I was slowly reaching for my wallet as I spoke.

"I suppose so," the woman replied after she had thought it over for a moment. "I think she has another spare room. Or maybe I could sleep in the same room as my daughter. But I could only afford a bus ticket for my daughter, and I don't know of an easy way to get more money since I lost my job here. I could get work near my sister's house, but I can't afford the bus fare for the trip."

She stirred her cereal again. I pulled out the cash I'd been given the previous morning and placed it on the table.

"Unless my math is off," I said to her, "after paying for my coffee, this will cover your bus fare and leave you enough for a meal along the way." The look on her face made me think of the old man, wondering if my eyes had been as wide when I'd found the twenty-dollar bill in my hand. She began to shake her head, and I pushed the money toward her.

"Please, take it," I insisted. "You need it a lot more than I do. For one thing, I've got everything I really need in my little canoe by the docks; for another, I only need to worry about me, while you've got a little girl who misses you waiting for you at the end of your bus trip. I know what it's like to feel lost and alone, and if I can do something to help another person overcome a similar problem, I'm going to do it. Besides, this isn't about me."

She laid her hand on mine and gave me a soft, appreciative look. I found myself looking back warmly, knowing I was doing the right thing. She ate her cereal with renewed vigor and was out the door with a hurried "Thank you" tossed over her shoulder.

I watched her go, as did my waitress, who poured me a fresh cup of coffee. "On the house," she told me, "and so is your breakfast."

Refreshed with hot coffee and warm eggs and cheese, I took the *Enterprise* back out to sea. I was back down to my original thin dime, but as I made my way farther south in the afternoon, the idea of a luckless mother sweeping her daughter into her arms still brought me a good deal of comfort and joy.

The weather was calm, but I already knew enough to keep my eye on the sky and stay close to shore. The last thing I wanted was to be caught in a sudden storm with no way of getting my bearings.

I was finding my way down the coastline with relative ease. I looked up at the sun and took a moment to reflect on how things had changed over the last couple of days. I had no idea this little trip would come to have so much meaning for me. It was so much more than a dare, a case of beer, and adoring groupies; something greater was definitely at work. The old man had helped me grasp it, and the luckless mother had confirmed it. I wasn't doing something on a reckless dare; I was touching lives.

I cracked open a beer and relaxed. It was clear to me the journey held a lot more in store for me in the days and nights to come, and at the time I was eager to find out what lay ahead of me. Had I known beforehand the events about to unfold, though, I would have sold the *Enterprise* that very night—or given her away—and started walking back home.

Chapter 9: **The Sound of Storm Clouds**

I will admit I fancied myself terribly clever when I studied the maps of the next part of my journey. I'd already had quite a few harrowing experiences taking my little canoe through the open ocean, and the appealing coastline of North Carolina seemed to present a variety of opportunities for avoiding those harsher elements. From my position in southeastern Virginia, I could take the *Enterprise* south through the Albemarle Sound, then directly into Pamlico Sound right afterward. It certainly looked like a shortcut at the time.

While I had carefully checked my route, I'd given only a cursory glance to the weather. I knew a storm system was in the works and headed in my general direction, but the prevailing winds were not favorable for a squall. It appeared the storm would pass either to the north of the Sounds, where I was currently resting, or to the south. But I figured if I took my time through the Sounds I'd still miss the storm.

Feeling invigorated by my choice of route and the seemingly favorable weather conditions, I struck out once again into the water. "Fearless" Fritz was once again on the move.

- Caught in the storm -

By my charts, I was crossing from Virginia's coastal waters into North Carolina's when the wind began to change. At first I didn't pay much attention to it. My power came from my arms, after all, not from sails. Then I felt the wind blowing harder and the waves growing all around me. With a sickening chill I came to grips with what was going on. The storm was coming right at me. I had paddled right into a natural ambush.

I tried to paddle faster and get more distance behind me before the storm hit, but all too soon thunder rolled and lightning split the sky above me. Compared to the predictions I'd seen in the morning, the storm's speed was alarming. The wind howled in my ears, and waves almost as tall as my shoulders, when they didn't merely break over me and leave me drenched, rose up to carry me aloft and slap me back down on the water. I'd rather have gone a couple rounds in the ring with a prizefighter than go through such a beating. The water slammed into me with tremendous force. I felt as if Neptune's fists were beating me to death.

After long hours of forging through the sheets of rain and wind, my voice hoarse from yelling at the elements, I came across an inlet I knew would provide some much-needed relief and protection from the storm. So I pulled my canoe on shore, made my way inland, and found myself at a small bed and breakfast situated by the side of the road. The elderly couple that ran the place took me in and dried me off, offering me hot tea and some of the leftovers from their chicken dinner. I could hardly refuse, and I thanked them over and over again, especially when they also offered to let me sleep in one of the rooms they had not rented for the evening.

I awoke the next morning refreshed and ready to continue my journey, delighted to see the rain had slowed and now only dark clouds chased each other across the sky. I asked my gracious hosts if I owed them anything, and they simply shook their heads "no" and wished me well on my trip. Apparently they'd seen a clip about me on the local news and were considering themselves lucky to be part of the story. I had a fleeting recollection of Paul as I headed back out to the inlet where I'd stashed the *Enterprise*.

I got myself back on a southerly course and tried to keep one eye on the clouds as I put more miles behind me. I stayed close to the coast and cut a bit more toward the east, closer to land in case I needed to find shelter again. I had the sense this storm wasn't done with me.

- The storm returns -

A few hours into the afternoon, I found out I was right. The winds shifted, and suddenly the storm was hitting me straight on. I had to paddle squint-eyed against the torrential downpour, which was actually coming at me more like sideways than straight down. I was back to using my sneakers to bail out the canoe.

Unfortunately, between the downpour and the rough waters, the sneakers weren't doing me much good. No matter how quickly I bailed or how efficiently I used the sneakers, the *Enterprise* was listing pretty heavily. Water continued to pour in, and it soon became clear if I didn't do something drastic, and fast, I would be swamped. I fought down the panic threatening to crawl up through my guts and looked over my canoe for ballast to dump.

My eyes quickly settled on the food and beer still in my canoe—I guess they must have weighed twenty-five pounds or more. With no other alternative, I started tossing it all overboard. I tried not to think about how much money I was throwing away or how hungry I was going to be in an hour. What mattered was keeping the *Enterprise* from capsizing and me from swallowing a stomachful of seawater. The bow of the canoe began to lift out of the waves as I tossed out the last can of beer.

After I had jettisoned the food and the boat was more buoyant, I turned my attention to calming down. I found it easier to relax between the waves, and I took the time to get my breathing and heartbeat under control. I learned to pace my breathing and my paddling with the crashing waves, which meant I had a few moments to calm myself down before steeling myself for the next onslaught of salty abuse. After a few waves, the realization hit me—I was proving the point I'd bravely made back in Allentown—canoes can handle rough water as well as bigger ships.

The storm lasted all night and into the next morning. While enduring its onslaught, I made a conscious effort during the whole time to move with the waves and relax between them, until I finally made it into Pamlico Sound. I kept the *Enterprise* on a southerly course. I could see a break in the clouds ahead of me, and I put more effort into reaching the first sunlight I'd seen since the storm began.

The wind seemed a bit stronger when I reached the edge of the storm, and more than one wave broke dangerously close to me. I didn't waste any time bailing out the canoe at this point. I decided I'd worry about emptying and drying the interior of my boat when I wasn't in the middle of a downpour. Despite the weary protests of my muscles, I paddled with the waves, and as I made it to the outer edge of the storm, the gale picked up alarmingly. But it was blowing in the direction I was heading, pushing me south at a better clip than I could manage paddling with no wind behind me. I used the paddle like a rudder to help stay on course for a while, relieved to be free of the storm's chilling grasp.

Once I was sure I was clear of the storm, I set about employing my abused sneakers to bail out the rest of the seawater from the canoe. I needed to find a place to head ashore and get some rest. I also needed to dry out my sleeping bag and the few MREs I had left after dumping so many things overboard. I looked over my shoulder at the near-blackness of the storm front and felt pangs of regret for ditching the ice chest and the beers I hadn't gotten around to drinking. But the choice had been to throw them overboard or drown with them. I missed the beers, but I was now extremely thankful to be alive.

Out of the darkness came a large, slightly rusted fishing boat. Unlike the small, one-man craft of the fishermen I'd encountered earlier in my journey, this was a large trawler, and as the crewmen went about the deck checking for storm damage, one caught sight of me and pointed. I didn't hear what he shouted, but I certainly heard the horn blast when they rushed to their starboard side to wave. I waved back and continued to scan for a place to put ashore. They passed me heading south, and I didn't blame them. They probably had things to fix after getting tossed about in the gale-force winds.

I finally found a dry strip of beach and pulled the *Enterprise* ashore, finally getting a chance to check for tears in her canvas hull. Thankfully, I found no severe damage, and all of the water still in her was from the storm. I dumped it out and left the canoe to dry, and then did the same with my sleeping bag. I lay down on the sand and fell quickly to sleep.

The next thing I knew, I was waking with a start in the middle of the night. My sleeping bag and canoe were dry, but I still felt almost completely worn out. Rubbing my eyes, I packed the sleeping bag back into the canoe and whipped up one of my last MREs. I was extremely hungry and ate faster than I'd intended, but I wasn't about to eat another. My supplies were limited as it was, and I didn't need to make matters worse by pigging out. I pushed the *Enterprise* back into the ocean, and turned myself south again.

I carefully made my way down the coast as the sun rose, emerging from Pamlico Sound and looking toward Morehead City. Ships of quite a few sizes were moored at the marina when I finally arrived there, including the trawler I'd seen yesterday. I tied up at the end of one of the piers and stepped up onto it easily, then headed for the seafood restaurant close to the pier. I walked inside, and was surprised when I saw someone waving at me.

- Captain Mike -

"Weren't you the cat in the canoe yesterday?" he asked. I blinked, and then quickly understood I was looking at one of the men who'd been on the deck of the fishing ship. I nodded my head "yes" to his question and introduced myself with a firm handshake. His name was Mike, and his friends were all members of the crew on what they informed me was a shrimping boat. Mike was the captain of the vessel. A couple of them had heard of me, and the next thing I knew I was chowing down on a huge bowl of steamed shrimp, clams, and oysters.

They must have known I was hungry, because a second and third bowl soon appeared as if by magic from the kitchen. By the time I was finished, I felt like I was going to explode. I took a deep breath and hoped I could handle all the seafood.

Mike clapped me on the shoulder with the bronzed, weather-beaten hand of a veteran fisherman. "If you like this kind of fresh catch rather than the processed stuff you've had until now," he challenged me, "I'll show you how to get it yourself. Come on, let's teach you how to fish."

They took me aboard a different boat used for sport fishing, and we headed out into the open ocean. During the course of the morning, Mike told me the Carolina waters were teeming with sea trout, flounder, bluefish, and striped bass. We were out at sea for about an hour, and then we headed back in close to the beach. Mike said while doing some shrimp trolling the last couple days they had been looking for flounder and bluefish up north, but after the storm the crew was a bit gun-shy. Mike told me I would like shrimping and if I was still around when they went out the next time I could go with them.

I learned a lot about the life of a sea fisherman and what it takes to make a living at it. It turned out to be a dirty job. I kept thinking how much easier it was in the canoe no matter what I went through. In the meantime one of the crew had made a huge breakfast, and with the motion of the boat I was getting a little seasick. After Mike gave me something for my stomach I was ready for more.

We ventured a bit further north, and Mike lent me a fiberglass fishing rod. While we'd been trolling, some summer flounder had apparently passed by us. So we cast our lines and promptly pulled some of this large species of fish into the boat. I was proud when I reeled in the first catch of the round, a mighty six-pounder. Mike complimented my skills, and I wondered if I'd make a fisherman someday. It was late afternoon by the time we headed back for Morehead, and I was in for a shock.

When I'd left it, the *Enterprise* had been floating serenely by the pier where I'd tied her up. When we returned, she was hanging from the pier, my oars and the other equipment scattered beneath it. I smacked my forehead, and the shrimpers had a good laugh on me. I'd forgotten I'd arrived at high tide, and, holding to a schedule established eons ago, the tide had gone out since we'd left on our fishing expedition. I hadn't left enough slack in the line, which is why it now hung in mid-air and moved with the breeze instead of the waves. I joined Mike and his crew at laughing at my mistake and considered it a lesson learned.

Mike let me keep the fishing rod, as well as the couple of the catch of the day, and then gave me more mullet for bait. Mike also gave me the name and address of a friend of his in the Brunswick, Georgia, area to go shrimping. I thanked him and helped the fishermen pull in their various catches to the seafood restaurant. But I got a bit worried when I looked again to the north. Apparently the storm wasn't done with the area. By the time the boat was empty, the tide was in again, and I knew I had to resume my journey before the storm returned with a vengeance.

Chapter 10: Silver Linings

Storms were continuing to harass the Atlantic coast. Before I'd left Morehead, a couple of weather services had reported tropical depressions forming in the Gulf of Mexico. It wasn't known yet if they'd form into hurricanes, but the outlook wasn't at all optimistic.

Had I gone back to Allentown to rest and recuperate for a while, which I was contemplating, I might have second-guessed the idea of continuing my journey. But at this point, I couldn't think of any reason to turn back. In fact, I had every reason to carry on. I was continually meeting members of the press, and it was clear my story was spreading, judging from how people were treating me—which was more like a celebrity and less like a curiosity.

Mike had told me his crew had originally shipped out of Brunswick, Georgia, but had come north for the flounder and sea trout. He told me Brunswick was called "the shrimp capital of the world" and I'd have no problem getting plenty of food in town or looking up and connecting with his friend. I thanked him for all of his help and waved good-bye to him and his crew as I put the *Enterprise* back to sea and began paddling south.

The crew had taken the liberty of emptying one of the buckets I'd filled and replacing the seafood with fresh ice and several cold bottles of beer. The other bucket was full of tasty food from the restaurant, and they told me to take both buckets with their blessing

By the time I was back out to sea and heading south, the weather was definitely changing. In the distance I could see dark clouds dominating the sky, and I knew I was heading right toward some awfully nasty storms that could easily turn out to be hurricanes. It was a far cry from the fair weather I'd had during most of my earlier excursions, the first day's suffocating fog and subsequent rainstorms notwithstanding.

But it wasn't the only change. I was clearly adapting to this life at sea, because my arms had become quite used to paddling. I was developing a good tan, and I had grown a beard. For the first time in quite a while, I felt alive. And while I wasn't quite sure where the journey would take me, the thrills and trials of the journey itself made the trip worth pursuing.

I spent the next day maintaining my southerly course. I was trying to stay close to shore in case the storms picked up again. The storm clouds to the south showed no signs they would head off in another direction, and I'd be lying if I said I wasn't worried I'd be going through another ordeal of bailing water with my buckets from the fishermen in Morehead City instead of my sneakers and dumping foodstuffs overboard. But they were a long way off and the sun was shining the entire day, so I took the opportunity to enjoy it as much as possible.

This meant, of course, going through about half the beers from Mike and his crew before putting in to a secluded stretch of beach and passing out.

Over the next couple of days, while I propelled my way through the waters bordering South Carolina, I took some time to note how extra nicely everybody was treating me, a relative stranger. On more than one occasion people in their fishing boats and yachts would wave me over to ask about my trip and offer me food, beer, and encouragement.

One gentleman in a brand-new cabin cruiser offered me the use of his vacation home on Hilton Head Island while he was enjoying "a life at sea" for a few days. I thanked him profusely, but I'll admit, the idea of staying alone in somebody else's house was a bit disconcerting. I had to wonder if he were really this nice and gullible to trust a complete stranger not to rob him blind, or if he were only acting and a rabid, man-eating bulldog might be waiting under the bed in the guest room to gnaw my face off at the first opportunity.

In the end, I found a party in Hilton Head and ended up sleeping in the hotel room of a friend I'd made, after he'd bought me three glasses of Dewar's and pressed me for details about how I'd weathered so many storms.

The next major stop I had in mind was still Brunswick, Georgia, because I was running low on the food I'd been given and the fish I had caught off of Morehead City, and I was curious to see the place Mike had told me was "the shrimp capital of the world." But I was in for a surprise on my way. The southern sky still threatened to unload all sorts of stormy unpleasantness in my direction, so I was focused more on maintaining my course and conserving the rest of my food than on the waters around me.

- *The manatee* -

Had my attention been on the latter, I probably would have seen the great gray mass speeding toward me before it slammed into the *Enterprise* and nearly capsized it.

I was wondering what was going on when it happened again, this time from the opposite side. It took most of the strength in my lower body to stay in the canoe, and I put down my paddle to steady myself and keep the boat level on the water. I was close to the shore, and people were running up and down the beach to point and shout at the impromptu show.

The creature slammed into my canoe a third time, and my blood ran cold when I heard something snap in the bow. I got my paddle out again and, hoping it wasn't a shark, gave the speeding gray mass a good prod for its curiosity.

As I turned the canoe toward the shore, I noticed the sea monster had paused and now was coming at me again. I gave it one more poke, causing it to rear, and I found myself looking into the dark and rather soulful eyes of a manatee. I got the impression the "sea cow" was merely curious about my boat and had simply been playing. Regardless of its motivation, the manatee now turned and headed out to deeper water.

I pulled the *Enterprise* onto the shore, and people swarmed around me. They all seemed to talk at once, saying they were sure it was a shark they saw in the water, wondering if I'd been scared, and giving me all sorts of stories about what they'd seen. I soon became more frightened of the potential danger they were describing than the actual playful misunderstanding I'd encountered.

I asked the beachgoers if I was near Brunswick, and one of them pointed down the coast, saying I was about a mile north of the city. I thanked him and took a moment to examine my canoe. Playful or no, the manatee had torn a hole in the bow of my ship, and the cracking I'd heard was the breaking of several ribs—not my ribs or the manatee's ribs, but the ribs shaping the canoe. They were broken in several places. The damage wasn't severe, but it was enough to make me think twice about putting back into the water.

I met a pretty girl who'd been packing up to leave, and she offered to give me a ride. She said her name was Holly, and she told me she knew where I could get some help.

- The red house -

The ride turned out to be a taxi, and the driver was a little put off by the idea of lashing a canoe to the roof of his personal means of income. But Holly was terribly persuasive, and before I knew it, I was standing outside a rather nice, if somewhat old and run-down, house not far from Brunswick. I then noticed my new girlfriend head toward a porch populated by other girls who waved at her while shouting greetings and asking who I was.

Given their general demeanor, which was nice, but bordering on flirtatiously lewd, and the way they were dressed, which was in a fashion designed to show off their bodies rather than conceal them, it didn't take me long to put two and two together to figure something out: My canoe and I had been taxied to a cathouse—a brothel. The proprietress called herself "Misty" and told me she'd heard of my exploits on the local radio show.

"Some of Mike's crew used to come here," she told me, "but most of them have gotten themselves married. Not that it stops one or two of them," she added with a wink. "Unfortunately we've had some problems with the house and haven't been able to afford to hire someone to fix a few leaks in the roof, and with yonder storm coming, I'm worried some of the girls are going to get soaked."

"How bad are the storms going to be?" I asked, focusing as much as I could on her interesting hazel eyes and not on the rather generous amount of cleavage pouring over her desk when she pored over some of her bills.

"Pretty bad," she predicted. "They don't have enough steam to be full-fledged hurricanes, but we're still going to get hammered over the next few days. We're short on space as it is, and I don't know where we're going to put Holly and Sally when the rain starts coming in."

"I think it would be silly of me to try and ship out again into a storm this bad, especially since my canoe needs repairs," I thought out loud. "Misty, I'll tell you what. I don't need much to fix up the *Enterprise*. If you help me get the materials I need, I'll patch up your roof free of charge. It won't be a professional job, but it might help keep Holly and Sally dry."

Misty took me up on my offer. "I'd really appreciate it, Fritz," she responded. "I'm sure we can find a place for you to sleep, even if space is at a premium."

I shook her hand, and we had a deal. I went with Holly to the hardware store, and we returned with several sheets of plywood, a canvas bag, a handsaw, and a few incidentals like nails and staples. I spent the rest of the afternoon securing some of the plywood over the holes in the roof while the sun was still shining and then had dinner with the ladies and was introduced to them all.

My sleeping quarters turned out to be in the basement, on my sleeping bag beside my canoe, which was held off of the floor on a pair of sawhorses. As I lay awake at night staring up at the walls of bare concrete lining the basement of this house of pleasure, it occurred to me that I had not been propositioned for sex—not once. I was beginning to think something was wrong with me. Maybe I needed a bath or some cologne.

The next day's skies were looking more threatening. I hurried around the roof patching up any more holes I could find, and Holly came back from grocery shopping with a caulking gun, which I used to try to put some sort of seal on my admittedly amateur roofing job. I apologized in advance to Misty if a later contractor might charge her for pulling the patches off, and she shrugged and said she was grateful for the help. After dinner I set about cannibalizing the canvas bag to patch the hole in my canoe's hull.

The thunder woke me the next morning, and, compared to the last few days of activity, the house was much quieter. I waited for the ladies to wake up, because it would have been rude of me to knock on their doors not knowing how much they were dressed, if at all, or who they might have in the room. After they were up, however, I took my equipment first into Sally's room, and then Holly's, measuring and sawing the patches to the correct size, then used nails and caulk to hold them in place. The leaks were pretty bad indeed, and a few of the girls came in with mops and buckets to help with the cleanup.

Apparently ours were not the only rooms being worked on. All over the house girls were washing windows, dusting and vacuuming, fixing chips in the paint on walls, and trying to get stains out of their carpets. This work was occupying all the girls completely—I had to make myself a sandwich for dinner. And then I went back to the basement to work on patching the cracked ribs of the *Enterprise*.

The next day's rain gave new meaning to the words "torrential downpour," and I was happy my canoe and I were indoors. My mood improved more when Misty told me the patches were holding up well against the rain, and she was therefore throwing a party in my honor. A few gentlemen had braved the weather to visit their favorite girls and were happy to join in. My memory of the details about what went on during the party are sketchy, but, needless to say, everyone enjoyed a fine time, and that night was one of the most restful and relaxing I'd spent on the journey so far.

By the time I woke up the next day, the rain had slowed to a light drizzle and sunlight was poking through the clouds to the south. I knew I should take the hint and get back out on the water, so I said good-bye to Misty, Holly, and all of the girls. They were sorry to see me go, but wished me well and invited me to come back anytime.

Holly got her taxi driver friend to take me back to the waterway. I wondered if any of them would talk to the press about my visit and my handiwork, then became somewhat worried Julie might hear about where I'd been. But I resolved if she ever did, I wasn't going to let it slow me down.

Thoughts about Julie hadn't crossed my mind in the last couple of weeks, but the possibility of her being upset did sour my mood a bit. However, spending some time in Brunswick lifted my spirits again, especially when I found the seafood restaurant where Mike got his start and still occasionally brought in a load of shrimp. By now I couldn't remember the name of Mike's friend, but it didn't really matter—it seemed like everyone knew everyone else in the area, and they were all expecting me! The owner of the restaurant told me Mike had called him and told him if I showed up he was supposed to take care of me. And he did—he gave me all I could eat and drink, as well as a place to sleep on one of the shrimp boats.

- The rugged-looking man -

The next morning I was approached by a tall, rugged-looking man wearing a black, snap-billed cap and knee-high rubber boots, his face weathered and deeply tanned. Pulling a pouch from his shirt pocket, he started to roll a cigarette. When he was finished, he lit it with the strike of a match off the wall. He then reached his hand out and introduced himself as "Captain John Martin—Captain John to my friends." As I shook his tough and callused hand, I noted he looked just like Mike had described him.

Captain John invited me to go on a day shrimp run. We drove to his boat, boarded, left port, and motored out to sea. Along the way he showed me everything about the boat and what it took to get it ready. It was quite an experience seeing and learning it all firsthand. The neatest thing to watch was how the shrimpers, after dragging them for about an hour, brought the drag chutes up and dumped them on the deck. The catch contained every color of the rainbow with all types of fish, crayfish, crabs, eels, and even some trash. The chutes were then re-lowered to start another drag. They sorted the shrimp by size, chose which fish to keep, and discarded the "trash" overboard.

The seagulls seemed to know instinctively that when the nets were being raised, it was their "chow time," and they appeared as a swarm overhead to catch the discarded fish, a lot of it in midair before it hit the water.

On the way back to port, the cook again insisted on making me something special, combining some crayfish, crabs, and shrimp. It was very good, but by now, thinking back over what I had managed to rustle up to eat on my trip so far, I started to wonder to myself, *WHERE'S THE BEEF?* That night back at the restaurant, sure enough, there was more seafood as well as beer. The next morning I stopped off to have some breakfast and to thank everyone for the good time.

I related some of my stories to the proprietor, and then, heading down the pier on which the restaurant was situated, launched the

Enterprise back into the water, headed out into the sea, and began to paddle south.

Before me spread the coast of Florida. I was full of confidence. After facing fogbanks, sharks, tropical depressions, and manatees, I felt certain I was ready now for anything. But I should have been paying closer attention to the lessons my journey had taught me, because it had truly shown me the unexpected is always closer than you think, and nothing is ever as easy as it seems. And the Gulf of Mexico would prove to be no exception.

Chapter 11: **En-Gulfed**

On my way down to Florida I met a man named Frank who was sailing from North Carolina to San Francisco. He was impressed by my attempt to make a similar trip in a canoe. His sailboat was a fine, tall ship, and we crossed paths several times as we made our way down the coastline. The only unfortunate thing about meeting Frank was the encounter with him caused to me deviate from my original course, which was to head through Lake Okeechobee to the west coast of Florida. I had originally planned to make my way from there around the Gulf of Mexico along the coasts of Florida, Alabama, Mississippi, Louisiana, Texas, and Mexico and from there south along Central America to Panama.

After we had spent a couple of days together, Frank decided to take his sailboat out to sea. I, on the other hand, wanted to stay in the Intracoastal Waterway. We made plans to meet in Fort Lauderdale at the Bahia Mar Marina. The Bahia Mar is the sister Yacht Club of the Great

Kills Yacht Club on Staten Island, New York, where this dare started. I knew if I made it that far, I would be treated well.

As I paddled along the waterway, I looked up at the sky and noticed a huge, black storm looming, and I realized it would soon come right over my path. I spotted a bridge just ahead of me where I knew I could get relief from the deluge. So I started paddling as fast as I could toward cover. I barely made it under the bridge when all hell broke loose. The rain was so hard I could hardly see twenty feet in front of me. As I pulled the *Enterprise* up on the shore I noticed a man sitting under the bridge abutment.

- "This is my bridge" -

"Pretty wet out there," he said. He was holding a bag in his hand, and I could see the top of a bottle sticking out. He was dressed in a pair of black baggy pants and his sneakers were full of holes. His tee shirt had a logo on it, but I couldn't make it out. His beard was about three inches long, and his hair was pulled back in a ponytail.

"Yeah, I just made it," I responded to his friendly greeting.

"Come on up and have a drink," he called. I was a little hesitant, but I didn't see anyone else around. The last thing I wanted was to get rolled by a bum.

I opened the cooler, got out a couple of beers and walked further up under the bridge. "My name is Fritz," I offered.

"Glad to meet you, Fritz," he replied. "What brings you out in this weather?"

I told him, "Oh, I'm on a dare."

"A dare?" he asked. "You mean someone bet you couldn't paddle your canoe in a rainstorm?"

I laughed and answered, "It's a little more involved than that. By the way, what's your name?"

"I'm Mark," he informed me, "and it is my pleasure to meet you."

"Pleasure is all mine," I insisted. I could see Mark was well on his way to blissful intoxication, and it was early in the day. I offered him a beer, and he took it, thanking me. We each opened our cans and drank a toast to "dares." We sat there for hours talking and drinking until it was almost dark. I was really getting drunk, and Mark was already there.

"Hey, Fritz," Mark suddenly blurted out. "Are you hungry?" I was so hungry I could have eaten a bear.

"Sure," I said.

"Come on then," he suggested, "I know a good place to eat."

I asked, "What about my canoe and stuff?"

Mark told me not to worry about letting it stay there and assured me no one would touch it. "This is *my* bridge," he said.

"Okay," I conceded, and off we stumbled up to the street. We walked about a mile and then went up an alley. When we went up the alley, I figured he was going dumpster diving, and I wasn't ready to eat from a trash bin. But then, to my relief, he opened the back door of a building, and we walked into a kitchen.

"I guess you do this all the time," I ventured.

He laughed and said, "I've never been here before."

"What?" I asked.

He laughed and said, "I know the owner, so don't fret. Go out front and sit at a table. I'll take care of everything."

I walked where Mark had directed me to look for a table and saw twenty or so men dressed the same as Mark. I thought I was in a soup kitchen or the back room of a church. As I swept my eyes across the room, I also saw people dressed in regular clothes eating and drinking. A young lady brought over a glass of beer, sat it in front of me and asked me what I wanted to eat. I told her I was waiting for Mark.

"I know," she informed me. "He'll be here shortly. He told me to take care of you."

"Bring me whatever you want," I responded. "I'm so hungry I could eat a bear."

She laughed and said, "I'll check on the bear."

"Wait!" I quickly called out to her as she was turning around. "I don't have any money."

"Don't worry," she assured me. "We take good care of Mark's friends."

Suddenly I heard someone begin to play the piano. I looked over and was surprised to see *Mark* at the keyboard. I couldn't believe my ears. He was playing classical music! I sat listening and couldn't believe it. He was great! How could a bum, living under a bridge, drunk as a skunk, just sit down and play so beautifully? The waitress brought me a large dish of meat loaf, corn, mashed potatoes with gravy, and two rolls with butter, along with a cup of black coffee.

"I couldn't find a bear. Will a turkey do?" she asked.

We both laughed, and I said, "Thanks." She walked away, and I ate my food. I had finally found the BEEF! After a while she came over and sat down and asked me how I knew Mark. I was thinking to myself, *Oh darn, here it comes. Now I'm in trouble.* I told her I had just met Mark about six hours ago. I asked her what her name was, trying to change the subject and get her off track.

"I'm Sally," she said. I shook her hand, and she asked, "Where are you from? I can tell you are not a southerner because of your accent."

"Accent? What accent?" I asked. She laughed. "I'm from up North."

"Where up North?" she probed.

"Pennsylvania," I confessed.

"What brings you to Florida and tell me, exactly how did you meet Mark?" she asked. I told her I was on a dare and I met Mark while seeking shelter from the thunderstorm. "What kind of dare?" she asked. I told her I was going from New York City through the Panama Canal by canoe and intended to end my jaunt in California. I told her my sponsor gave me only a dime—a dime was to make a phone call when I get to California or to call if I quit the trip.

"So that's you!" Sally exclaimed. "I saw you on the news about a week or two ago. I never thought I would run into a real-life adventurer or someone who was that stupid." She laughed and grabbed my hand. "I'm only kidding," she quickly added. "I think it's great you have the confidence to prove you can do this."

Sally left the table and came back with another beer. She sat down and told me she thought I was an amazing man. She said anyone who has the guts to travel alone in a canoe into the Atlantic Ocean and come out in the Pacific was okay in her book.

- Mark was a neurosurgeon -

I asked her why a man with Mark's talent lived under a bridge. Sally told me that Mark had been an accomplished neurosurgeon practicing in one of the largest hospitals in the northeast.

"He was operating on a young boy," she explained, "using a new, experimental procedure, when suddenly something went wrong. His young patient died, and Mark could never pick up a scalpel again. Feeling terrible for the boy's death, he closed his practice and wandered all over the East Coast. He ended up here about four years ago. Now he plays the piano for his food and booze."

Sweeping her hand over the room, she continued, "All the guys you see here are friends of Mark's. What he gets in tips, he gives to the other guys to pay for their food. Many people come here in the evenings just to have drinks and listen to Mark play."

After telling me Mark's story, Sally asked me where I was going to spend the night. I told her "I'll be under the bridge with my possessions." She said she had room and would love to have me stay with her. I really wanted to, but I was afraid I would go back in the morning and find nothing. I asked for a rain check, and she gave me a kiss on the cheek.

"Have a safe trip," she whispered. "I'll be praying for you."

I went over to the piano where Mark was playing. I sat down beside him on the bench and listened. "Not bad for a bum, eh?" he joked.

"Not bad for anyone," I said. I thanked him and told him I was going back to the bridge. I promised him if I ever got back his way again, I would look him up. I inquired, "You're not going to change your address, are you?"

Mark laughed and said, "Thank you for your seed of life, and God bless."

Some time later I met up with Frank in Fort Lauderdale at the Bahia Mar Marina. After enjoying a week with Frank at the marina, and finding myself on TV as well as the front page of several newspapers along the Florida coast, I needed to get the show on the water. I found it difficult to justify parting ways with him so soon. I sat down with Frank over beer in Lauderdale, and we went over our charts. We re-drew my course, and he adjusted his as well. We decided we would work together, continuing down the Florida coast to Key West, then cut across the Gulf to the Yucatan Peninsula of Mexico. It was a decent plan, and the more I worked with Frank, the more I appreciated his company.

We caught and ate shrimp and lobsters, living like kings for the better part of a month. I didn't mention to Frank I considered him good luck—while we sailed together, the tropical depressions deep in the Gulf never developed into hurricane-scale storms reaching Florida to slow me down any more than I already had been.

Unfortunately, our arrival in Key West brought with it an unexpected turn. Frank got a telegram from a family member in San Francisco saying his father was deathly ill and he should return home immediately. Without the money to pay for a plane ticket, Frank worried he'd never see his father alive again. After a long discussion, I helped Frank determine the best alternative: to sell his boat. This proved to be more difficult than it sounded, though, because he was not the sole owner of the boat, and he knew he would stir up legal problems if he tried to sell it.

Finally we came up with a plan. I would try to use my local fame and trademark charm to find someone interested in buying a part ownership in the vessel. In only a few days, I was fortunate enough to find such a person. It turned out the buyer I lined up was a collector of boats and well known in yachting circles, which made the other joint owners comfortable with the deal. Frank was enormously thankful to have linked up with him and agreed to a very reasonable buyout price.

As I saw Frank off at the airport, wishing him and his family well, I was happy he would be with his loved ones during a time of sadness. At the same time, it suddenly hit me that Frank had convinced me to alter my original route *around* the Gulf to a course going *across* the Gulf, but now I would have to do it solo—without help from Frank, a daunting task, to say the least.

- Meeting Carl Kiekhaefer -

But Key West held another bit of good fortune for me—it was there I had the privilege of meeting Carl Kiekhaefer, the owner of Mercury Marine Corporation. The occasion was the offshore powerboat race week, and we crossed paths at the Pier House Motel where the powerboats were docked and Mr. Kiekhaefer was staying. I was camped on the beach next to the motel dock using my canoe as shelter. When we met, he asked me what I was up to, so I told him about my trip. He must have thought I needed a break from the sea, because he offered me the job of driving him around Key West to all his appointments for a couple of days. He also very graciously rented a room for me at the motel.

Carl and I quickly became very good friends, and I will always remember how generous and personable he was to me. One of the last things Carl told me before we parted ways was to give him a call if I ever needed help with the rest of my canoe voyage or any future endeavors. I didn't know it at the time, but later Carl Kiekhaefer would play a big part in another of my future fearless forays into the wild.

During the drama of Frank and his boat, my canoe was drying in the Key West sun. Our adventures down the Florida coast had reopened the seams I'd sewn in the canvas patch I'd applied in Brunswick, and as a result the *Enterprise* was acting more like a submarine than a canoe. It took a long time for her to dry out, and when she finally dried, I tried heat-sealing the patch on before sewing new, sturdier seams. By this time, Thanksgiving was upon me, and I resolved not to impose on anyone's family gathering despite the invitations I received.

- Thanksgiving dinner -

One family I met, though, wouldn't take "no" for an answer. I'd met them in a bar on the island, a young husband and wife with charming personalities. Out of nowhere, the couple pulled up in a van alongside the curb where I was walking from a hardware store. They insisted I get in and come along with them. Since I already knew these folks and was definitely curious, I got into the van. During the short ride to their place they picked up a few other people, and in a brief conversation I learned none of the other people going with me had family on the island.

The sun was setting before we arrived at the couple's home. The mingled aromas of oven-roasted turkey, marshmallow-stuffed sweet potatoes, and freshly chopped cranberries greeted us when we entered. They had gone all-out to prepare a huge Thanksgiving meal, and had invited all of us specifically because we didn't have family of our own in Key West with whom to celebrate the holiday. The feast was much bigger than the one I'd had in Morehead, and was in fact the biggest meal I'd ever had until then. But more importantly, it felt like a family gathering. Within an hour I knew everybody's name, and everybody knew me. People were all over the house, eating and drinking, laughing at jokes, and having a great time.

After I fixed the hole in the canoe, I had still other preparations to make before trying to cross the Gulf, an endeavor most of the Key West natives were convinced was impossible. Their negative attitude, however, only encouraged me to take my planning more seriously. I took two lengths of PVC tubing, put caps on the open ends, sealed them with polymer cement, and attached both to the *Enterprise*. They would serve as pontoons, stabilizing her in the rough waters. My equipment was checked, re-checked, and sealed for seaworthiness.

Finally, I talked to the local Coast Guard station and went over with them an extended forecast for the next two weeks. As far as they could tell, the wind patterns were not likely to spawn more tropical depressions but looked favorable for me to attempt what one of them called "a completely featherbrained and totally reckless idea."

Two weeks of clear weather, a fully repaired and stabilized watercraft, and supplies to last throughout the four-hundred-mile journey seemed to be good enough. November was coming to an end, but the weather was unseasonably warm and sunny. I figured this would be a good time to leave. I put the revamped *Enterprise* out into the Gulf's waters and waved good-bye to the folks who came down to the shore to see me off.

My first day in the Gulf was uneventful, filled with my usual paddling and steadying and stopping to eat twice. But after some of the challenges of my journey this far, an uneventful day was okay with me, and in fact my spirits were lifted. It differed a lot from the treacherous first day of my journey and heightened my morale.

When I woke up in my canoe the next morning and saw dark clouds above me, however, it was an entirely different story. My first instinct was to question the weather patterns I'd studied with the Coast Guard a few days ago. *But,* I rationalized, *they're the Coast Guard; they should know what they're doing, right?*

- Thirty-five-foot swells -

Then the seas became choppier and the waves grew higher, and my confidence in the *semper paratus* guys from Key West started to wane. Only twenty-four hours earlier I had been using the bait from my bucket for a little casual fishing, but by the time lunchtime rolled around I had jettisoned the bait and was frantically using the bucket to bail out my canoe. While the bucket worked a bit better than my sneakers, these waters were an entirely different animal than I'd faced before, and they seemed intent on sinking me.

Suddenly, through the swiftly escalating wind and crashing waves, came the muffled voices of other men. I looked and saw a sailboat rushing toward my port side. The crew called out to me and made gestures for me to head in their direction. Some of them were already producing ropes and life jackets. I sized up their boat and quickly calculated they didn't have enough room onboard for both the *Enterprise* and me, and I wasn't about to leave my boat behind. It was a difficult decision, and it brought me to tears, but I had to scream at them to go on without me.

Between my gestures and continued bailing, the captain seemed to understand my intent, and he called to me the one sentence I wanted to hear loud and clear over the stormy seas: "Help is coming! I promise!"

Then, quickly, they were gone. And I couldn't have felt more alone in the wide-open vastness of the Gulf if I'd been suddenly locked in a supply closet on Mike's shrimping boat. With every passing minute the wind grew more powerful and the waves around me crested higher. The *Enterprise* and I were tossed around like a cork in a fountain. I was jostled around in every conceivable direction, and I'm certain the Gulf came up with some new ones to try out on me. I was completely disoriented and getting more terrified by the moment. In the space of a few seconds I went from riding high in the air on top of a swell to dropping unceremoniously between solid walls of water that looked like they were about to close in around me and seal my fate forever.

Later, after what seemed like an eternity to me, a powerful foghorn cut through the sounds of the wind and the waves. The distinctive white hull of a Coast Guard vessel cut through the swells, and at the same moment something cracked loudly under me.

Several men in life jackets and one already wearing scuba gear came down from the deck on safety lines and started wrestling me and my equipment out of the canoe, then struggled to hoist up the canoe itself. I could tell immediately the keel was broken from the way the hull was bending. It was like seeing a beloved pet with a fractured spine. She was still in one piece, but for all intents and purposes the *P.S. Enterprise* was dead. The crew told me the swells were over thirty-five feet high and I was lucky to be alive. I didn't feel lucky, though. I felt defeated.

Chapter 12: "That Walk"

Andy wasn't much help. I got him on the phone as soon as we got back to Key West. I told him everything I had experienced, including how I'd repaired the canoe myself, only to have the Gulf snap its keel like a twig. I could hear the disappointment in Andy's voice when he finally spoke; it was like a cell door slamming shut.

"Fritz, I'm sorry to admit this, but I've been worried about you. Every time I heard about you on the news or read about you in the paper, I was happier about the fact you were alive than worried about our dare. You went a long way, and a lot of people are proud of you. But I'm going to say this as your friend and sponsor: Come home. Leave everything and come home before you get yourself killed trying to take me up on an impossible dare—I'd feel awful if something happened to you."

Andy must've said something to Julie, because she unexpectedly called me within an hour and told me she was coming down to Key

94

West to see me. To my surprise she flew down the next day, and we stayed at the Pier House. The friends I'd made at the Thanksgiving dinner were sympathetic enough to lend me money for airfare home, so I immediately bought a plane ticket. They also graciously took my broken canoe into their basement and offered to store it for me until I could get back. While I was helping to carry it down the stairs, I spotted a red wig among their various belongings. I asked them if I could have the fake hair, because I didn't want anybody to recognize me when I arrived back in Allentown after my dismal failure. They agreed, and between the crazy wig and my beard, I felt I had a pretty convincing disguise. As it turned out, Julie and I ended up with tickets for the same flight, so we flew back together to Allentown. I donned sunglasses and a floppy hat before getting off the plane—Julie thought I looked great. But she was still living in New Jersey, and she needed to get home as soon as possible, so she just dropped me off at the Ale House. My first desire upon returning was to get seriously drunk and forget about the whole ordeal.

I arrived at the Ale House half an hour before its normal opening time of 11 a.m. I was half expecting to see Andy when I went in. Instead, I ran into my old friend, Norman Morris. I had a hunch he wasn't about to give me the time of day, but not because of my failure. Norman had a problem with "long-haired hippies." I went inside and took a seat at the bar. He walked up to me and looked at me closely before informing me the bar wasn't open yet. I waited until opening time finally rolled around and was able to get one of the other bartenders to serve me a drink. Some people I recognized came in around noon. I overheard them say they were stopping in for a celebratory round of drinks before heading off to the wedding of another real good friend of mine, Stephen Bell. I was happy to hear my friend was getting hitched, but I wanted to remain incognito. Nobody seemed to recognize me, so I figured my disguise was working.

- Bobbie recognized me -

I soon felt nature calling, so I set down my drink and made my way to the men's room. I noticed Bobbie Loudenslager, another one of my friends, talking to Norman. After a short pause, I heard Bobbie yell out, "Hey, Fritz! What's with the hat? Don't think you can fool me—I'd know that walk anywhere on earth!"

I suddenly heard Norman laugh at the top of his lungs. "By George, you're right!" he exclaimed.

I turned around and, with a smirk, threw my hands in the air as if to surrender. Immediately I heard a chorus of cheers, and my friends mobbed me. I'd forgotten Norman had seen me with a beard before. It's why he hadn't kicked me out on sight before his official opening time. My buddies bought me a few shots of Dewar's and convinced me it would be a real treat if I went along with them to the wedding just as I was—in my borrowed wig, sunglasses, and hat.

- Stephen's wedding -

We drove over to the Muhlenberg College Chapel, where the wedding was taking place, and caught the end of the ceremony. When I finally got through the receiving line and put my hand out to them, Stephen actually turned to his new bride and asked, "Who's this hippy?"

Looking kind of puzzled she said, "I don't know, I thought he was one of *your* friends."

"Hello," I said, and pulled off my wig and sunglasses. He recognized me right away and gave me a huge, welcoming hug. He hinted to me it might be more fun to blow off his own wedding reception to celebrate my return home, but with his new bride standing next to him, he confessed he was only kidding. Yet, there was a brief moment when I sensed he wasn't kidding at all and would have rather been out "partying" with me.

Realizing that I had not been invited to the wedding, I thought I might just give my best to them and "bug out," but, being the good friend he was, Stephen insisted I go to the reception festivities. It turned out to be quite an elegant affair, and I was questioned by many other friends, acquaintances, and guests there that evening who were curious about my adventure on a dare.

Stephen was also quite excited that I had made it back to Allentown and seemed quite pleased that I had come to his wedding, even though I had come on the spur of the moment and incognito. As a matter of fact, he insisted that the photographer include me in the wedding pictures in a pose with his new wife and him, one with the wig and hat, and one without. I was totally amazed at the hospitality of true friends.

The only awkward feeling I had during the entire wedding experience was when I sensed the disposition of Stephen's new in-laws—they didn't seem entirely thrilled by my attendance. But except for that uncomfortable sensation, I realize as I look back on my memories that open-minded individuals are more likely to remember the best of times much more clearly and easily than the worst of times.

The wedding and reception turned out to be a nice time of respite from my concerns and a joyful reunion with my friends. I might have been repressing some of my fears about my quest, and I was delighted to find myself in such a relaxing situation without really planning it.

The next few days I made the rounds in Allentown, still disappointed in my failure, but heartened by the jubilation of my friends. I finally caught up with Andy at the Ale House about a week after I'd flown home, but it was quickly obvious he wasn't interested in helping me return to the Gulf. Norman listened in on the conversation while he wiped down the bar, and after Andy left, he slid me a beer and told me it was on the house. As I drank, he asked me a few questions about the Gulf.

- Norman to the rescue -

"All in all, it sounds like you were doing the right things in the wrong places," he surmised. "Do you think it can be done?"

"Absolutely," I replied, "provided my boat doesn't get snapped in half again."

"Grumman has an aluminum canoe with a lifetime guarantee against breakage and tears," Norman informed me. "If I were to get you one of those puppies, would you want to go back?"

"Yes, yes!" I cried, jumping off of my stool. "I don't want to give up and let this challenge go undone if I can help it."

I had to curb my enthusiasm for a few months, however. Norman gave me a full-time job for the winter at the Ale House—not exactly the best place for a habitual drinker to work. The dream took a back seat for a while, and my life became rather humdrum. I worked, got drunk, sobered up, then worked, got drunk, and sobered up again.

David Gross had a rental house in town where I was able to stay awhile. He allowed me to do some remodeling there to help pay the rent. I wish I could remember all the things that went on, but everything was hazy. Dave knew some Eastern Airline stewards that stayed at the house from time to time, and that opened the door to some good parties. There was always something going on—if not at the Ale House or the King George Inn, then at Andy's, Stephen's, Phil's, Eddie and Augie's, or Dave's place. The winter of 1970–71 seemed to drag on forever.

Then after a couple of months, Norman decided it was time to take action, and he made it happen. One spring day a truck showed up at the Ale House with a brand new Grumman aluminum-hull canoe strapped to its roof. Crisp black letters stenciled on her bow proudly stated her name: "*Miss Allentown, PA*." Norman also gave me a new camera and a lot of other supplies to replace what I'd lost in the catastrophic storm. The local press exploded with the news—**"Fritz Hasn't Given Up!"** Frank Banko, owner of a local beer distributor, added his name to my list of sponsors, along with Norman's company; Mack Truck; and Jake Papay, owner of Queen City Tires, a local tire company.

Apparently Norman and Loretta had done a lot of legwork to obtain the support of these companies and some other people who became financial contributors by promoting my trip to all their associates in Allentown. Andy's dad, "Attorney Perkin," sent a letter securing the support of my United States representative, the Honorable Fred Rooney. To my surprise, Congressman Rooney came to wish me luck in person. When he shook my hand, he presented me with a unique gift he had obtained for me in Washington—a permit granting me passage through the Panama Canal to use when I arrived at the locks in my canoe!

Then Norman went the extra mile—he flew back to Key West with me to make sure all my equipment arrived. He also accompanied me to the Coast Guard station to get some of my other personal items and a fresh weather report. I stayed tight-lipped about my opinions of Coast Guard weather predictions, but Norman made it a point to go over the weather patterns and my "float plan" several times. And on top of all the other things he did, he insisted on buying me a new radio with enough range to get weather reports all across the Gulf. When everything had arrived, he insisted on coming to the pier along with the press. I thanked him for everything—and all he did was smile.

"Finish what you started, Fritz," he told me. "Good luck, and Godspeed."

Chapter 13: **The Republic of Cuba**

I felt the hint of a gentle, refreshing breeze when I left Key West for the second time to head out into the Gulf of Mexico aiming for the Yucatan Peninsula. As I took the *Miss Allentown* further out into the open water, the breeze quickened slightly. We had fitted the canoe with a nine-foot sail to catch any brisk eastward winds, and I used my paddle as a tiller. I maneuvered the boat so the sail would catch the wind and overcome the Gulf Stream, which would have propelled me back to the Florida coast.

It was definitely a lazy day—a lot nicer than the nearly disastrous day of my first attempt in the *P.S. Enterprise*. Night came, and the wind died away with the sunlight, so I lowered the sail and paddled for a short while, then stretched out in the canoe to get some sleep.

The sea was utterly calm and peaceful the next morning, as smooth as a plate glass window. I paddled around for a bit before I stowed the oars and let myself drift so I could enjoy a beer and a bite to eat. After my meal, I paddled a little further and checked out my surroundings. Thankfully, I saw nothing but blue sky and blue sea. This was fine by me after some of the rotten weather I'd already encountered on my journey. The problem with it, however, was I had no idea how far out I'd gone or where I was on my chart,

I lay back in the canoe, stretched out, and looked up at the sky. Out there I found total relaxation, offering me the opportunity to reflect on life, and I grabbed the opportunity by the horns. Little things I'd forgotten about a long time ago came back to me. I mulled over in my mind the events of this whole trip, and indeed my entire life, and took a long, hard look at myself. Here I was, traveling alone on a perilous journey on a dare with my friend. Once again, I had to ask myself, *What am I trying to prove?* I still couldn't come up with an answer. I gave it some serious consideration through the afternoon and into the evening, with little success.

- Surrounded by whales? -

For the longest time while I drifted, lost in my reverie, I didn't hear a sound other than the gentle breeze and a few small ripples turned up by the ocean current. Then, out of nowhere, the boat moved by itself, perpendicular to the current! I could tell immediately this was not a wave action—something had definitely bumped into me. Immediately I concluded, *Shark!* I bolted upright and grasped the aluminum sides of the canoe, bracing myself. Then I noticed an odd noise. It wasn't the same sound the sharks had made, nor was it the ocean breeze. Unluckily for me, the sun had already slipped past the horizon, and I was enveloped by darkness.

Suddenly I heard a sound off to my right, a wet exhaling of air, which sprayed into my face. The canoe was bumped again, and I gripped the metal tighter. Then came some splashing off to my port side followed by the same odd sound. The spray hit me again, only from the port side this time. In a minute I identified the spray—it was coming from blowholes. I was surrounded by whales, or manatees, or porpoises, or dolphins! At least I think they were whales or some other large mammals—I never actually asked them what they were.

For some reason, these gentle giants scared the stuffing out of me. I wasn't really fearful they might try to attack me like sharks would, but I really didn't want them to come up under me and playfully flip my things and me all over the Gulf. I lowered myself into the *Miss Allentown*, perhaps thinking the hull would offer me some sort of protection. I fumbled around until I found a length of rope and tied myself to the canoe. Another giant something bumped the canoe, and I craned my neck to get a look at it. But I still couldn't see a thing—I couldn't see six inches in front of my nose.

"Leave me alone!" I shouted at them. "Whatever you're doing, knock it off and get lost!"

The boat rocked again, and of course because I was hidden, I couldn't tell what was going on. After a bit more jostling, another spray of seawater came down on my face. I spat and cussed and yelled more imprecations at them. I also called out to God to help me. Then after a few minutes of quietness, it became clear to me the school of whatever they were had finally left. Slowly, I untied myself and sat upright in the *Miss Allentown*. I looked up and saw the sky wasn't completely black—the stars had come out, scattering tiny diamonds all over the sky's velvet blackness. I wasn't alone.

For a long time, I mulled over what had happened. The more I tried to figure it out, the more I came to understand something beside the playful leviathans was with me. I hadn't talked to God since I'd left Paul, the old man who gave me the twenty-dollar bill, but now seemed as good a time as any. I was thankful for the way He had guided me through this situation and other far more perilous jams in the past. I found myself apologizing to the sea creatures I'd cursed out. I looked up at the starry sky and extended my arm, as if I really could take hold of His hand and shake it in thanks.

The next day came and brought with it a lot more heat. I pulled out my tiny radio and spent some of its precious battery life to get a weather report out of Key West. It was in the upper nineties on land, and I didn't need to be a weatherman to tell it was hotter out here. The sunlight reflecting off the calm water was heating the interior of the *Miss Allentown*, and everything inside was getting warm. If I had packed cut-and-bake brownies, I could have baked them right there on the spot, in the bottom of the boat. I bailed some water into the canoe (now that was a switch!) to try to keep the beer from getting too warm and exploding.

Every once in a while on a day like this, when I let the canoe drift, I sometimes slipped over the side of the boat into the water. As much as I would have enjoyed a long, leisurely swim in the cool water naturally trapped a few feet beneath the surface, I didn't indulge, because I could often see fins not too far away. This day I sensed something more sinister than whales might come snooping around. I stayed in the water only long enough to get wet and cool off, then hopped back into the hot metal of the canoe.

I repeated this process several times throughout the day, careful each time, of course, not to capsize the canoe and mix my food supplies with the briny Gulf water. After every dip, I cracked open a beer, took a swig of Dewar's and lit a Camel cigarette, thinking about home and the people I missed. The lack of wind caused the smoke from my cigarette to hang in the air above me, lingering, hazing over the sunshine and making small curls in on itself. The more the day wore on, the more I noticed the mirror-like sheen of the calm waters and the perfect blue of the cloudless sky. When the sun eventually sank beneath the waves, broad bands of color emerged in the west, painted by an unseen hand.

- A light in the distance -

When the darkness of night closed in around me, I thought for sure I saw faint a light in the distance. For a moment, however, I considered the notion I might have heat stroke and might be seeing things. I dipped my hand in the water and splashed it on my face. I sat in the canoe and let it carry me closer to whatever it was in the distance. As I got closer, I knew beyond a doubt I wasn't seeing a mirage at all—I could clearly see a light in the distance. I picked up my paddle and headed toward it. A few hours later, from the way the light beam was positioned above the water, I figured out I was looking at a lighthouse.

I wasn't really sure where I was, but in short order the *Miss Allentown* drew up onto a sandbar. I stepped out of the canoe and walked across the embankment to a place where I could easily climb up for a better view. I was thankful for the easy climb, because after three days with little exercise, my legs were screaming in pain. I was standing on a little curl of land which was separating me from the lighthouse—and what I figured would be a warm meal and a decent place to sleep. I stepped down from the embankment and got back in the canoe, excited to see what was waiting for me by the lighthouse.

I guided the canoe around the land; the sea initially carried me away from the lighthouse and then turned into an eddy, which put me back on track. I was looking forward to meeting the lighthouse keeper, and, somewhere in the back of my mind, I entertained the idea that he might have an attractive daughter. I ran a hand through my hair and tried to prepare myself for meeting new people, but I was completely unprepared for what happened next.

- *"American! American!"* -

Out of nowhere came the loud report of a gunshot. A flare, burning red as blood, rose into the sky and illuminated several figures standing on a high ridge. They were carrying weapons, and two of them raised their arms. Then I saw two flashes from large muzzles, and two loud cracks ringing through the inlet sending two crimson flares through the sky. I heard another sound, this one a string of staccato shots, and bullets whizzed by me no more than a couple of inches above my head and into the water behind the canoe. I dropped my paddle and raised my hands in the air.

"American! American!" I shouted.

Some of the men on the shore picked up my yell and shouted to each other with clipped, foreign speech I didn't recognize. I was hoping and praying the guy who had shot at me with the machine gun wouldn't lower his aim.

I wasn't sure what scared me more: the initial gunshots or the heavily accented voice echoing my shouts of nationality. Two more shots rang out, and two more red flares lit the night sky. More men were running across the ridge, lining up along the sea wall. I could tell they were loading and checking their weapons. A few of them began to point and shout, while others made gestures in my direction. They were waving their hands up and down with their palms down.

I wasn't clear on what was going on. I honestly thought they were waving at me. So, I smiled and waved back. Again an assault rifle fired on me in response. I saw the muzzle flare followed by splashes of water off the side of the *Miss Allentown*. I threw my hands up again.

Finally, I put the pieces of the puzzle together. I now knew where I was and why I was being shot at. The language I'd heard was Spanish. I was off the coast of Cuba!

A moment later, two more flares suddenly dispelled the darkness again. I took the time in this light to notice Cuban flags on the shoulders of the soldiers' uniforms. I had been moving slowly toward the shore before, but now I was paddling shoreward as if my life depended on it—because, unless I was greatly mistaken, it certainly did. I didn't look away from the line of soldiers as I closed in on them. I was scared, but they didn't need to know it.

I paddled up to the sea wall. One of the soldiers, holding his rifle on me, stepped down to rest his foot on the aluminum hull of the canoe, trying to tell me either where to go or what to do. However, since I could not speak Spanish, I had no idea what he was going on about. He put weight on his foot, and it slipped. Obviously, the soldier had never dealt with a canoe before. One of the first and hardest things you learn when you're learning to handle a canoe is how difficult it is to get in or out of the craft when it's sitting in the water. And this was not the wood and canvas of my first canoe, the *P.S. Enterprise*. The *Miss Allentown* was crafted from smooth, sleek aluminum—slippery-when-wet aluminum.

The soldier went face first in to the water. His weapon went flying from his grip, and he splashed about to my starboard side. Some of his compatriots were laughing as another one of them stepped down toward me, more carefully, using one hand to steady himself on the seawall as he tried to climb into the canoe. The second he let go of the wall, however, he slipped off too, this time to port. I tried my best not to laugh, but kept the canoe afloat and looked from one soldier to another.

A third soldier had the bright idea of jumping into the water first, and then trying to crawl into the *Miss Allentown.* He hauled himself up, and then put one foot on the hull. As soon as he tried to stand, his foot slid away from him, which resulted in him doing an impromptu split directly on the canoe! His face made a comical expression, and he slid off the canoe without protest, holding his crotch in pain. Finally, another soldier laid his rifle down, slid into the water and crawled onto the canoe. He was careful, and pulled himself right up to me. He managed to get into a cross-legged sitting position, and I felt a chill go down my spine as he drew his pistol and put it to my head.

Did he think I'd done something to make the canoe super slippery? Perhaps he thought I'd been jostling his compatriots on purpose? Either way, he was barking at me in Spanish, which did not help my comprehension of the foreign language at all. He made a gesture to starboard, however, and it was clear he wanted me to paddle in another direction. I didn't have to be told twice.

As calmly and carefully as I could, I paddled us as directed, until I came to a small beach. The canoe slid onto the beach, and the Cuban soldier grabbed me by the collar and hauled me out of the *Miss Allentown* without any explanation. Rough hands grabbed my arms, and I was shoved down to the sand. They still had guns to my head, so all I could do was look up and helplessly watch them plunder my canoe. I had to bite my tongue when I saw my camera tossed carelessly from one soldier to anther, before it was finally torn open and the film yanked out. They were kind of excited to have found my two cases of beer and the Dewar's. They quickly cracked open a few cans of American brew and began passing them around to each other.

Finally, after the soldiers had gutted the boat and strewn my belongings all over the beach, they hauled me up to my feet and marched me to the lighthouse. Once inside, they drew straws to determine the watch order. One of them handed me a couple of pieces of bread with ants crawling over it. To my disgust, the ants were not crawling on the sandwich by accident; they were the meat of the sandwich! As hungry as I was, though, I had no choice but to choke it down.

Early the next morning, the butt of a rifle prodding me in the temple awoke me. A small gunboat was moored near the lighthouse. The soldiers, my canoe, and I became the boat's cargo for the day. Our journey was a short one, and for me it was doubly confusing because of the language barrier and the circuitous route we traveled. About a half hour after we left the lighthouse, we got hung up on a sandbar. We sat silently for a few minutes before I stood up, with their rifles still pointed at me, got off the boat, and showed them how to free themselves from the obstruction.

The captain of the boat helped me back onto his vessel and showed me my can of OFF mosquito spray. The day had grown sunny, warm, and quite humid on the water, and the little insects had grown in both number and annoyance. He made gestures as he talked, indicating he wanted me to use it. I nodded, taking it and spraying the back of my neck. He was amazed at how quickly the insects began to leave me alone. I looked around and saw that both he and the soldiers, despite the hot weather, were wearing long-sleeved shirts buttoned up to the neck. Clearly, they were used to this problem. The captain, however, yanked off his shirt and doused himself with the insect spray.

The rest of the ride was uneventful, lasting the rest of the day and all night—uneventful, of course, except that I under arrest in a foreign country with a language I couldn't decipher. Exhausted by my ordeal, I dozed off.

Once again, I was rudely awakened by a rifle butt and marched off the boat and into the presence of more soldiers and a couple of officials wearing suits. These soldiers joined the squad who had pulled me from the water, making about a platoon by my estimation. We piled back into the gunboat and continued on.

By late afternoon we arrived at another stop, where the platoon swelled to a company. And now we were traveling by truck. Our next stop was a small base where the officials got out and talked. I was pulled out of the truck and put into a car with two guards on either side of me in the back seat. Another truck pulled up, and I counted the soldiers as they climbed into the trucks—about 350, enough for an entire battalion. We traveled down a dusty road with one truck in front of us and one behind us. We stopped at a small Army base, and more soldiers joined the caravan. Finally, I saw a sign I understood: "Havana." We were entering Cuba's capital city!

- A sickening smell -

We stopped outside a squat, concrete building surrounded by a chain-link fence topped with barbed wire. I was pulled from the car and escorted inside. It smelled like a men's locker room, and the place was not in good repair. I was then led down a hall to my new quarters. The dingy walls of the hallway showed evidence of several leaks in the ceiling and lots of dirt, dust, and large stains. They were solid enough, however, to squelch any idea of trying to escape. As we walked, I was almost overcome by an awful, sickening smell. I was pushed into a little cell which measured, I would estimate, about six feet by twelve feet. I found the source of the smell—a hole in the corner with an accumulation of urine and excrement was the culprit. I was confined in semidarkness, and the little air available was almost impossible to breathe. Flies, mosquitoes, and roaches infested the room.

By now, I had gathered the situation was pretty serious and my best chance for survival was to cooperate. I had done nothing wrong, as far as I could tell, and I simply had to wait until I could explain my trip to someone in a position high enough to make a decision to allow me to continue on with my journey.

The next couple of days were a lot lonelier than any I had spent at sea up to this point. Three times a day they slid me a plate of stale bread, and something looking like grits along with a cup of rather rancid water. It was so bad I needed extra water to wash it down. I think they gave this to me as a joke. I was being treated on the whole with a sort of contemptuous neglect. I tried to look at the evidence from their viewpoint and considered what they had found in the canoe: two life jackets, two sets of maps, two canteens, and two paddles... Was it possible they had come to the conclusion that I had transported someone onto Cuban soil and was using the innocent tourist act as a smoke screen?

It was not at all reassuring when I indeed heard by way of the grapevine from one of the guards a few days later Fidel Castro was not a happy camper when he found out someone from America had landed on his island without being detected.

Chapter 14: **Fritz Sprandel, Secret Agent?**

A couple of days later I got a visitor. He was a short man with close-cropped, dark hair and clear brown eyes. When he spoke, it was not in Spanish, but in heavily accented English.

"Are you Fritz?" he asked me.

I looked up and nodded affirmatively.

"Ah. My name is Leopoldo Gonzalez, and I have been assigned to you to act as your interpreter. Please stand; they are going to move you soon. This is only a temporary inconvenience."

I was taken to an interrogation room. On the walls were pictures of Fidel Castro with a submachine gun.

- "CIA? Me?" -

Some time later the room was invaded by several plainclothesmen. The first thing they asked me was, "Who is the other person and where did you drop him off?"

"What other person?" I quickly replied. "It's only me," I assured them.

With this I pulled out a pack of Camel cigarettes and offered to share them. They all took one.

"Again, what's your name?" they demanded.

"Fritz Sprandel," I answered.

"Our United States contacts tell us prior to leaving the States you were in contact with the CIA and the FBI," one of them said.

"How long have you worked for the CIA?" another asked.

"CIA? Me?" I responded incredulously. "Get the heck out!"

The agent screamed back at me in an extra loud voice, "No more lies!"

I can't remember how long this went on, but it seemed like hours. They finally gave me back to Leopoldo to take me to my next destination.

"Thanks," I told Leopoldo, standing up and moving toward the door. "Where am I being moved to?"

"A holding house for other criminals from outside Cuba, like yourself." He said this without contempt, as the door slid open.

"But I'm not a criminal," I protested as I was escorted out of the cell. Leopoldo fell in step behind us.

"Please forgive me, I am telling you what I am told," my interpreter told me as I was loaded into another truck for the journey to the holding house. As pleased as I was to talk to someone who understood what I was saying, the fact that I was being put in with "criminals" didn't sit well with me at all.

According to Leopoldo, Castro had chosen a holding house situated in a block of houses inside the city limits under the jurisdiction of a CDR (Committee for the Defense of the Revolution). Everyone in the house was under strict twenty-four-hour surveillance. People living in CDR communities were special, with access to more food and sometimes refrigerators, televisions, and phones.

July was now right around the corner, and with it came the major Cuban revolutionary national holiday. Cubans were getting ready to celebrate. Christmas and other religious holidays had been outlawed. Since religion is the opiate of the masses, an all-out war was being waged against God and his believers. July 26 had become a holy day for Cuban communists. Children were taught to revere it, anti-communists to fear it, and Marxist-Leninists to worship it.

Leopoldo had explained to me why he spoke such good English: He played baseball so well in Cuba the White Sox had recruited him to play third base in Chicago. But when the revolution broke out, he decided to return home to Cuba to be with his parents and the rest of his family.

We passed several brand-new-looking tractors but with farmers working up a sweat right beside them. I asked Leopoldo about them and why the farmers were still working the field by hand.

"The tractors are from Russia," he told me, "but nobody in Cuba knows how to use them. So the farmers continue to do their work by hand. The tractors, they sit, because nobody is sure how they move. Anybody with any brains fled and went to America, with no one left to teach us. This is how many things are different between our countries," he explained.

- Labor camps -

"Over on the right," Leopoldo pointed and said, "is an agriculture labor camp. As soon as a person is contacted by a relative in the United States, he or she is viewed by the communist regime as a political outcast and is sent to a labor camp."

Leopoldo talked on and on about the labor camps and how the people in Cuba, and especially in labor camps, had no rights. "Men and women, young and old, white and colored, national and foreigners," he continued, "have to perform the hardest tasks without adequate food or clothing or medical care." I could see Leopoldo's eyes watering while he talked. It was probably because he already knew he would have to endure placement in a labor camp to get back to the United States.

I nodded, indicating my understanding of what he was telling me, and thinking about the ways things were different back home. I felt a definite pang of homesickness as I looked around the truck at the soldiers and their automatic weapons.

Leopoldo then told me he was going back to speak with the Swiss Embassy, one of the few embassies on the island, about my plight.

- The seven men -

We soon arrived at the holding house, which was in a block of row homes in old Havana. After being admitted by the front room clerk, I was led into a room occupied by seven men. I recognized them all— Chico Miles, Raymond Johnson, John Marcus, Luis Frese, Gabor Louis Babler (the red-bearded, Hungarian monk), John Davis, and Lester Perry—all seven of them Communists or Black Panther sympathizers. I had seen them on TV or read about them in the newspapers. They were all also on the FBI's "Most Wanted" list. The seven men shared several things in common: Each knew his return to the United States meant immediate arrest; each knew neither Russia nor China would admit him into their country; and each still wanted freedom—from any nation in the world that would grant it.

The seven were fugitives. They were killers, dope runners, plane hijackers, and armed bandits. For more than a year they had been held in the same building in Old Havana where there were bars on every window and door, and guards watched them almost constantly. Each was allowed out of the building for a walk on his own a few hours each night. I shared the lot of this rather select group for fifteen of the forty-five days I spent in Cuba.

The door slammed behind me, and I looked from one face to another, full of uncertainty and fear.

I now had plenty of time to reflect on my unfortunate plight while confined to the same building in which the seven fugitives were being held. A couple of scary questions haunted me. Would I ever have a chance to tell my story to my customers back at the Ale House in Allentown? At least one of these men had killed someone without giving it a second thought. Would I be the next one on his list? I didn't belong with this group. I knew it. And they knew it.

I found myself on the alert all day—and especially vigilant when darkness fell. Sleep came slowly for me, but it was a light sleep. I heard every sound in the building and imagined a lot of others. I tried to stay awake and analyze every one of the men. What made them tick? Did they accept me, albeit slightly?

Chico Miles was the quietest of the group. He was a friend of Angela Davis and had hijacked a plane. All he did was sit on a bench by himself—he was a real loner.

Raymond Johnson was a bodyguard for a Communist leader in the western part of the United States. How he got into Cuba was a mystery. He was tight-lipped about it and stayed to himself for the most part.

John Marcus started fights just for the sake of fighting. He had once tried to kill himself by banging his head against the floor. He also slashed his wrists a couple of times. The others surmised he was crazy, and I had no reason to think otherwise.

Luis Frese was the talker. He got things done because he spoke fluent Spanish. A dope runner, he had broken out of jail in Texas and then hijacked a plane.

Gabor—that's the only name the others ever called him—explained to me why he was known as the red-bearded monk. A robber, he once stole a police car and then escaped from jail by disguising himself as a monk while a group of monks was visiting the prison. The others referred to him as "the brownnoser." He was a wheeler-dealer with the guards, constantly currying favors from them using his incessant, persuasive talking.

John Davis stole a boat in Florida and fled from the country. No one knew what he was trying to escape.

Lester Perry boasted he had killed seven persons—one of them by mistake! He told me he had taken part in a Brinks armored car holdup and had also derailed several railroad cars.

All seven had time on their hands. They were not allowed to do any work to occupy themselves. One day was exactly like another, and the time hung heavy for them in their cells. And their confusion seemed to mount with each passing day. Each one was a Communist sympathizer and in a Communist-ruled country; yet, as one of them put it, "We're treated like dirt. We came here looking for asylum, and now we find ourselves prisoners."

Perry told me he weighed 220 pounds when he reached "Castro's paradise." That was before he got a rude awakening and found out people who hijack planes to Cuba are thrown into solitary confinement—a four-by-eight-foot concrete room with a cot and a hole in the floor. A lanky fellow, Perry wasted away to 130 pounds before they let him out of his tomb-like incarceration. Then he was able to bounce back to 170 pounds.

I got off on the right foot with Frese and Perry when I was thrown in with the group. Luckily I was able to keep some of the equipment and supplies from my canoe with me, so I could use the goodies as payment for a few favors. I gave them some of my clothing and other items made in America. It was the first new clothing they had seen in a year.

The crowning glory came when I mixed a batch of powdered orange juice concentrate. They absolutely loved it and couldn't get enough of it to drink. They hadn't received anything but milk or water since the beginning of their confinement. It wasn't Scotch and soda, but it was new for them. And anything that made a new day different from the previous day was worth celebrating. It was amazing how a simple treat like an orange drink will loosen a guy's tongue—even tough hombres like these seven.

Frese at one point felt free enough to talk about how he almost botched the hijacking of his "flight to freedom." One of the few times he relaxed his guard during the fifteen days I was with him, a smile on his face actually turned into a few chuckles as he recalled how he had to run across the airfield to catch the plane. His revolver, tucked under his belt, worked itself loose and slid down his pant leg, he told me, and he had to stop dead in his tracks to keep it from falling out onto the runway. Another few seconds fumbling with the gun, he admitted, would have made him miss the plane.

Davis, the mystery man, was a constant thorn in our sides. We could stomach Gabor and his bargaining with the guards, and Marcus, who seemed to be off his rocker. But Davis was a real fink. He'd fabricate wild stories and try to get the whole group in trouble. He'd sidle up to the guards and whisper about an escape attempt in the works. Or he'd tell them there was a plot under way to kill certain guards.

Fortunately for us, the guards quickly saw through Davis's phony stories and confined him to the building. At point, an idea floated among the group suggesting they should get together and "rub out" Davis. But cooler heads prevailed, and the men concluded nothing could be gained by reducing their number.

Normally, I was told, prisoners of the Castro government were put to work in the sugar cane fields—but not these guys. Boredom was their main punishment. Perry told me he became so tired of his routine, do-nothing days that he pleaded with the guards to let him go to work hacking sugar cane. "Not a chance," they told him. And they weren't about to change their minds.

Perry tried to convince them he was sincere in his request. He went on a hunger strike for fifteen days, he related to me, hoping they'd see it his way. All he accomplished by refusing food, though, was a lot of misery and a huge weight loss.

Perry wasn't the only one driven up a wall by the dull life. Any change in the routine, no matter how slight or unexciting, would have been a welcome relief to the men. At least they would have had something new to talk about. But they had no such luck.

Each day started at 7:00 a.m. with breakfast. And breakfast was always bread and hot milk. On days the guards decided they didn't have enough bread for themselves, we'd wind up with just hot milk. After breakfast, we'd be allowed to leave our twenty-by-thirty-foot home to take a walk up the block in groups of two. Nothing ever changed in the block, but at least we got a chance to stretch our legs.

Then it was back to our rooms again. And what did we do for the rest of the morning? Nothing—we'd merely lie down in our bunk or on our army cot and wait for lunch. The Cubans had no imagination. Lunch consisted of black beans and rice day in and day out. There was always a pudding and very infrequently a chunk of meat.

It was fun and games in the afternoon. We'd sit around the table and play cards and chess. Or, if we wanted to be different, we'd play chess and cards—anything to break the monotony. I often wondered how the old women back home managed to avoid going berserk playing bingo every night, night after night. The guards could have cared less if we were bored. They knew we weren't going anywhere and weren't about to try something stupid to get out. They just stretched out in front of their television set on the other side of the railing dividing us.

By American standards, Cuba's afternoon television programming left a lot to be desired. The only thing on the tube was a news program, and it was strictly Castro's propaganda day after day. After a while, we could recite the grandiose reports by heart: How glorious life was in Cuba; how Cubans were reaping the benefits of Communism; how sugar cane production was improving compared to the previous year's record; how important it was to remain vigilant to protect their island country, including detailed instructions on how to quickly disassemble, clean, and then reassemble their ever-present rifles and submachine guns. It went on and on, grinding out the themes Castro wanted his subjects to digest.

Then it was time for another nap, and finally, mercifully, dinner arrived at 5:30 p.m. And what was on the menu? Surprise, surprise— black beans and rice all over again. If we were lucky—and it didn't happen very often—they'd throw in a small piece of sausage or some other scrap of meat. After a while, the black beans and rice monotony reminded me of our American joke about bologna: You can slice it thick or thin, but it's still bologna. Like a one-note melody, there's no difference with black beans and rice. Add sausage or any other meat, and it's still black beans and rice.

Cuban television really blossomed at night. We could sit there with the guards and watch old Laurel and Hardy movies... or W.C. Fields movies... or American films dating back to the first, primitive days of U.S. television. More often than not, however, knowing we couldn't stomach the old shows as a steady diet, the guards would allow us to take a walk into town in groups of two again.

As boring as the walks soon became, they were still a relief from watching an old movie the third or fourth time. Surprisingly, the guards didn't accompany us on our walks—we left on our honor! We were instructed to return by 10:00 p.m. for lights out. And we always made sure we got back on time.

Things in the outside world didn't change much from night to night. No matter where we went, there were lines of people queued up—long lines at restaurants, long lines at theaters, and long lines at stores selling whiskey. But it didn't make any difference to us because we weren't about to buck any of those lines.

We quickly discovered how wearing the uniform of a soldier in Cuba had its benefits. It didn't take much convincing for the Cubans to step aside when a soldier—with a rifle or submachine gun slung over his shoulder—decided he'd like to go to the head of a line. That rifle brought the same quick results that slipping a ten-dollar bill to a headwaiter or usher brought back in the States. And there was no complaining on the "island paradise" when there were soldiers around. Each soldier seemed to embody the law himself, acting by himself as judge, jury, and sometimes executioner.

I can remember one night seeing a long line outside a spaghetti restaurant. An army truck rolled up, and a few soldiers hustled a man out of the place and tossed him into the truck. No one protested! Later I found out the cause of the excitement. A customer from the restaurant told me a soldier didn't like the way the fellow had complained about the lack of sauce for the spaghetti. And there was no doubt—that hapless guy was a goner. No ifs, ands, or buts about this situation; it was either life in the sugar fields, solitary confinement in some dungeon, or some rifle shots shattering the night's quiet.

Every once in a while, we'd be attracted by the loud noises coming from a community rally and would go to see what was happening. There were always large, enthusiastic crowds assembled by the time we arrived. The excitement never failed to materialize, of course, when army trucks rolled up one after another and spilled out their cargo for the rally. Soldiers with weapons sway even the strongest minds, at least in Cuba. No matter what the message at one of these events, there was always loud applause. Anyone who did not clap or cheer would disappear, led by the point of a rifle, and be loaded onto a truck.

We joke about the canned laughter on American television with its laugh tracks. Well, the Cubans take it one step further. They position sound-system trucks at these rallies to blast out recorded clapping. And, of course, all the people feared what would happen to them if they didn't get into the spirit of things when the sound trucks went into action.

There was always one fringe benefit on our outings. Cuban girls were friendly to American guys and had no reservations about inviting someone into their room, even if only for an hour. If a man was an American, the girl figured he might turn out to be her ticket to the U.S. some day. And they aimed to please, never mentioning money. But there was that 10:00 p.m. curfew back at the prison, and we didn't want to miss lights out!

- The "Fight of the Century" -

As the days passed, however, it was clear all these men were less interested in making my life miserable and more interested in obtaining information about the United States. I told them what I could, and in exchange they told me things about Cuba. For example, fourteen eyebrows arched on the men surrounding me as I started telling them about the "Fight of the Century" at Madison Square Garden on March

8, 1971, when Frazier landed a left hook in the fifteenth round that sent Ali careening to the canvas. They didn't know Frazier had won a unanimous decision as he handed Ali the first defeat of his pro career. A flood of questions broke out: How many knockdowns in the fight? Was Ali marked up at all? Was Ali over the hill after his long layoff? Was Ali still his old cocky self after the fight?

- "The easiest thing in the world to do is to be a communist in a free country ..." -

Things soon got more friendly, and they openly disclosed to me the United States media had offered Castro a ton of money in order to spend a couple of hours interviewing them. Castro had refused. Back in the United States, everyone had pretty much assumed these men were welcomed in Cuba with open arms as heroes or like royalty when they arrived. I was surprised to find the exact opposite was true. In fact, Lester Perry, former head of the Communist party in the United States, told me himself, "The easiest thing in the world to do is to be a communist in a free country; but don't try to be a communist in a communist country." The more they talked, the more I was fascinated by this shift in my perceptions, and the less certain I became that I'd make it out of where I now found myself.

Apparently, Castro had no desire for "these troublemakers" in his country and was holding them without trial. It seems Castro didn't want to share his role as the "Chief Rebel Troublemaker" on the island, because it was the role that had brought him to power in Cuba.

The food was a little better in the CDR holding house. In addition to the regular beans and rice, the people could get some rice with a little fish and occasionally some meat. I learned later it was cat meat!

Lester Perry explained to me this is why you would never see a stray cat or dog in Cuba.

Over the next few days, while Leopoldo waited for his chance to talk to someone in the Swiss Embassy, he came by to talk with me about Miami. He missed his old stomping grounds and was hungry for news from the States. He repaid my tales with what little news he had and brought me some of my items the soldiers had confiscated from the *Miss Allentown*: a compass and swim gear, then my sunglasses, and some of my maps and charts of the Eastern United States coast, the Gulf, and the Central American coastline down to the Panama Canal. It turned out these things were considered luxuries in Cuba, and as Leopoldo passed them to me, he told me the guards would want them—not to confiscate, but to keep. My cellmates agreed and offered to hide them and bribe the guards because they were planning an escape. In exchange, confident I'd get out on my own, they gave me information I could use to get some of the money the media had offered to Castro.

After returning from one of our jaunts out into town one night, we had just settled down into bed when we got an up-close look at Cuban justice. The soldiers brought in a prisoner at rifle point. He looked like an American, and the guards had locked him up by himself in a separate room. Suddenly a volley of shots rang out somewhere near the building. The next morning we asked the guards what had happened the night before and what all the shooting was about, but for a long time got nowhere with our questions.

Eventually, one of the guards loosened up and told us our visitor had attempted to dig the bars out of the plaster in his room. Such an action was a no-no, he said, and this meant the perpetrator immediately faced a firing squad. We were given a couple of days to reflect on the sudden departure of our visitor.

Finally, after I had spent a week in the CDR holding house, Leopoldo told me he'd finally spoken to a Swiss ambassador, and the result had been a little shocking.

"I actually spoke to him three days ago," said Leopoldo, "but at the time they figured you were just trying to get a free plane ticket home."

"That's absurd!" I protested, grabbing at the bars of the cell.

"That is what I told him," Leopoldo replied. "I told him you had already paddled this far and were not afraid to continue paddling. Finally this morning, I was told they are trying to work with the Cuban government to get you back on course. If it works out, you will go across the Caribbean Sea to Central America." I was very pleased to hear this.

- Suspected of being a spy -

The next day, Leopoldo came by with more news, this time from home. The United States knew I was being held without trial. Their brilliant idea was to capture some Cuban fishermen off Key West, Florida, and then trade them for me. It made me feel like a pawn in an American-Cuban chess game. Leopoldo didn't think this was likely. He intimated I was suspected of being a spy.

Another several days went by before I found out what the end result of all the negotiations would be.

Then it was my turn to leave the building. The guards told me the time had come for my trial in Santa Clara, about 175 miles away. On the heels of the execution we had heard, all I could think of was the sound of the rifle shots echoing outside the building. Fortunately, I was lucky!

Leopoldo and a few of the guards came to fetch me from the house, and this time I was put in a car and was told I was being extradited back to the province where I had first landed on Cuban soil. We took a rather windy road, and twice we took side turns to keep us on a back road, rather than taking a more central road.

Finally, we arrived at a huge building. It looked to me like an old Spanish castle out of a spaghetti western. It turned out we were in Santa Clara, the capital city of Villa Clara, the province in which I had been captured. Through the gates and ornate doors was a vast reception hall with chandeliers hanging from a vaulted ceiling. Leopoldo walked with my guards and me until we met a tall, slender woman in a suit.

"Fritz, this is Olivia," he said by way of introduction. "She will be your attorney before the Revolutionary Tribunal trial. She will be presenting the evidence claiming you are simply traveling as you have described."

I was about to ask why she wasn't telling me this herself, when she turned to Leopoldo and spoke rapid-fire Spanish. He replied in a similar way and then looked a little apologetic. "I am sorry, but I am not allowed to go with you. Everything has been explained to Olivia, and she will do her best to defend you. She unfortunately does not speak English, so you will not be able to converse with her."

"I understand," I said to Leopoldo, although I didn't. He left me with Olivia, with whom I walked into the large trial chamber. It looked full, with people in every row of seats watching me walk in and clearly unhappy with me intruding in their country. I think the people were curious and came to see an American in the courtroom. Olivia and I sat in front of the spectators. At the front of the room was a long table, behind which several men in military uniform sat. Judging by their medals and the amount of brass on their collars and shoulders, they were rather high-ranking officials. But the biggest surprise to me was the table in the middle of the floor between the officers and us.

Setting on the table, laid out neatly from one end to the other, were several maps and charts, a snorkel set, and sunglasses. I recognized every item—they were all the things I'd been given while living back at the holding house and had, in turn, given to one of my cellmates, who had promised each item would be well hidden. Clearly, their idea of bribing the guards had not worked out quite they way they had intended. I sat next to Olivia with the sinking feeling I was in a great deal of trouble. I had no idea what was happening from this point on and throughout the entire day, because deliberations went on in Spanish. I said nothing.

Finally, the military officer slammed the gavel and made some sort of announcement, in Spanish, of course. I was led from the room by the guards, and Olivia stayed behind. Leopoldo met me outside of the doors and walked with me.

- *"You have been convicted of spying"* -

"The tribunal has ruled you came here with the intent of spying on us," he summarized for me. "The evidence of your maps and charts was simply too strong for them. You have been convicted of spying. You are charged thirty thousand American dollars, and you will be held indefinitely."

I was too overwhelmed and terrified by the whole experience to say anything. Leopoldo looked sympathetic, but I was led away by the guards, who blindfolded me as soon as I was outside. I had no idea where I was going, or how I would be able to come up with thirty thousand dollars to get home. As a matter of fact, at this point, I wasn't entirely sure I would ever get home at all.

Chapter 15: **Alphabet Soup**

The United States has long had a policy of refusing to negotiate with terrorists. And on top of that, I'm sure paying someone like Castro thirty thousand dollars for a somewhat foolish adventurer because the United States was holding a few Cuban fishermen for questioning seemed tantamount to blackmail. I can't say I blamed the government for taking the stance they took on the matter, but I couldn't help wondering if I'd become a bargaining chip in some greater political game I wouldn't understand until I was sent back to America, if I ever managed to get out of Cuba.

These were all thoughts I had on the bumpy ride following my trial. I couldn't do much else but think, considering I was blindfolded. I knew I was in a car because the sounds around me were too close to belong to a truck, and more than likely I was being driven to some sort of prison facility far from the major population centers. As we motored along, I kept trying to remind myself I had done nothing wrong and all they could do was hold me indefinitely. Knowing these men with machine guns were within inches of me, however, didn't help my efforts to remain calm or hopeful.

Leopoldo tried to be sympathetic. While we drove, he talked to me and tried to keep me cautiously optimistic. We talked in a low tone of voice about the situation. Clearly, if the United States shelled out for my extradition, they could be forced to pay for every American who ever got in trouble in Cuba. They'd start hemorrhaging money directly into Communist coffers, and I could name about a dozen senators off the top of my head that would absolutely loathe such an idea. I repeatedly asked him where we were going, and he calmly reassured me I'd be fine. Unfortunately, given the country I was in, I couldn't take him at his word, despite how helpful he'd been since the ordeal began.

Finally the car lurched to a halt, and my captors pulled me out. They removed my blindfold, and I found myself standing outside a modest villa in the middle of nowhere. The car pulled away, and the guards ushered me inside. Another guard was waiting for me inside, meaning I was to be kept under surveillance by three men, not counting Leopoldo. He told me up front he would be staying only long enough to teach me how to communicate with the guards, and I couldn't blame him. The landscape was bleak, and a twenty-four-hour rotating watch of men with automatic weapons isn't my idea of a fun time either. As the prisoner, however, I had to learn to live with the conditions.

Over the next week, Leopoldo taught me how to do basic things like how to ask for food or to use the phone. For the most part, we were left alone, simply watched by the guards. Some of them spoke a little English, which made things easier. When Leopoldo left, I was sorry to see him go, but the guards and I were learning to live together. One way we interacted was by playing dominos. They taught me how to play the game by showing me the basic and more advanced moves, which didn't require much talking.

- My Bulova watch -

Another week or two dragged by without any noteworthy events. During this time, I noticed the guards always made it a point to rag on America whenever news came in. Of course, I played into my pride as an American and did my best to defend my country, although the only weapons at my disposal in my situation were words. One thing I observed was the way they constantly stared at my watch when I talked and gestured, and especially when I took my time making a move in our games of dominos.

The watch was a Bulova, an oceanographer's diving watch Norman had given me. It was waterproof to a depth of 666 feet of water and, as far as I could tell, it was indestructible. I finally figured out what the guards were trying to communicate. Some time during the third week of my stay at the villa, they started showing me their watches, cheap, Russian no-name wristwatches. "American, no good," they said, pointing to my watch; and then pointing to theirs they would assert, "Russian, good!" After three days of this I looked at the Bulova, wondering if a watch waterproof to a depth of hundreds of feet could take a little practical testing to prove American craftsmanship was superior.

At noon on the fourth day, we were out on the back porch of the villa, eating lunch and playing dominos. The sun was shining, and one of the guards elbowed his friend while he lowered his sunglasses and pointed to my watch. "American, no good... Russian, good!" he declared for the umpteenth time. He was grinning ear to ear, and his friend chuckled. I got up without saying a word, and his face fell instantly, unsure of what I was about to do. Looking him in the eye, I removed my watch very slowly, and then, without warning, dropped it onto the hard cement of the patio, and stomped on it three times for good measure. Then I kicked it through the open patio door, secretly enjoying their winces when it flew out. We all rushed after it. I got to it first, held it up, took it over to a basin full of water, and dropped it in. I crossed my arms and put on a smug look. The guards looked at each other in bewilderment, unsure of what to do next. After a few minutes, I reached into the basin and pulled out my watch, making a show of putting it to my ear. Indeed, it was still ticking away as if nothing had happened. I finally cracked a smile and held it up to my guards' ears.

"Americana, *primo*," I concluded, making a point of using the Spanish word for "good." Then I pointed at his and blurted out, "Russian, *no good.*" I've never seen a more furious man in my life. For a brief moment I was afraid he might go ahead and shoot me out of spite. However, all he did was angrily yank his watch from his wrist and, in the same manner I had, dropped it to the floor. Clearly, Castro did not equip his guards with oceanographer-grade timepieces. His watch shattered on impact, scattering tiny gears and springs every which way. I nearly fell to the floor myself, I was laughing so hard, watching the guards scramble about like they were acting out a vaudeville routine trying to retrieve all the miniscule pieces.

Needless to say, I got into quite a bit of trouble for such a stunt. It wasn't my last, but over the next few days I got the better of the guards on more than one occasion. They didn't have my rather skewed sense of humor, however, so it was never nearly as funny to them as it was to me.

Finally, one afternoon after I'd been incarcerated in the villa a couple of weeks, Leopoldo returned. He looked happy, and he patted my arm when he saw me.

"I have good news," he told me. "Our governments have reached an agreement. Our fishermen will be returned to us in exchange for you, and your fine was lowered from the 30,000 to 2005 American dollars. The money was wired to us this morning by a man named Norman, who says he is your sponsor."

I was thrilled to hear my old friend Norman had been pulling for me the whole time I was locked up. But Leopoldo wasn't finished.

"Clearly something is going on," he continued. "You are going to be flying to America with a few refugees from Cuba. Most people in your position are flown to Nassau in the Bahamas first. Why you have been given a direct flight, I do not know. But you will leave on the first available direct flight to Miami, Florida."

I was so elated I actually wanted to hug somebody, so I hugged Leopoldo, my faithful interpreter and friend, who had stood with me through my ordeal. I received the news initially on July third. The fourth and fifth passed without any activity because of the U.S. holiday. Finally on the sixth, I was put in a car, this time without a blindfold, and driven to a small airfield not far from the villa that had been my home for about fourteen or fifteen days.

When I arrived, I passed an area bordered by a barbed-wire fence surrounding a long queue of Cuban refugees waiting for passage to the freedom of the United States. I was driven past them, and then past a line of tanks between the terminal building and the tarmac where the plane was waiting. A couple of the vehicles appeared to be anti-aircraft platforms, and the huge machine guns atop them were fully as intimidating as the cannon on the tanks. I'd never heard of Castro shooting down a plane full of his own people as they left for America, but I didn't put it past him.

I was led onto the plane and taken to a seat in the back. I was the first one aboard, so I got to watch the refugees file in. No one spoke.

It was quiet enough to hear a pin drop, and I could feel their fear. Apparently it had occurred to them, too, that their freedom was assured only as long as they trusted Castro. The last refugee came aboard, and the door was closed behind him. The plane began to taxi down the runway, and I watched the refugees nervously peer out their windows at the military hardware as it began to speed by and eventually fell away when we took flight.

I have never seen a more rapid or drastic mood swing in a group of people than I did in those refugees. When we left Cuba on the short flight to Miami, they were frozen in their seats, silent and numb with fear. But as we approached Miami, however, they were up out of their seats, conversing excitedly and pointing out the windows at the wonders of their new home. They were absolutely in awe of the sprawling city they could now see glistening like a jewel-encrusted treasure in the afternoon sun.

- Overjoyed to be in America -

The plane touched down, and they couldn't get out of the cabin fast enough. The children, especially, were gleeful and excited to experience everything their new home had to offer. I was deeply moved and had to fight back the tears welling up in my eyes watching these people literally kissing the ground and so incredibly overjoyed to be in America.

Then two men in dark suits and sunglasses entered the plane when I moved to get out of my seat. One identified himself as Agent Johnson; the other said he was Agent Smith. They displayed their official FBI identification badges while they explained why they had been sent to interrogate and transport me: They needed to know everything I had seen and heard during my incarceration. For this debriefing, they informed me, I was being moved to a secure location. Next, the plane taxied to a hangar where I was escorted off and ushered into a dark-windowed sedan. From the hangar, we drove to a house in Miami where more men in suits awaited my arrival.

Secure location or not, it was clear I had, for all practical purposes, been moved from one house arrest to another. This time, however, instead of three Cubans, I was swimming in an alphabet soup of my own government.

Agents of the FBI, CIA, NSA, and later the ATF showed up and began to ask me a series of pointed questions. They wanted me to tell them all my impressions of Cuba, Castro, and Cuban military strength. They asked me for my recollections of any Cuban daily life I had been able to observe and also about the people from the United States with whom I was jailed. I was thoroughly grilled on every aspect about the Americans I had talked to—how they felt they were being treated, their hopes of being released, whether they regretted fleeing to Cuba, how long their hair was and how it was parted, how they walked and talked, and even how they held a cigarette.

To be honest, this is what I had expected—prior to my trial, one of my fellow prisoners had told me he'd worked for both the FBI and the CIA before fleeing to Cuba, and he had told me exactly what happens when a political refugee is freed from Castro's regime.

After some intense interrogation, Agent Smith told Agent Johnson how Radio Havana had leaked the story of my release and reporters were demanding a press conference to find out where I was. At this news, I blessed Norman and breathed a sigh of relief when they agreed it was time to let me go. They laid out the floor plan of the Captain's Lounge at Miami Airport, showed me where they'd be, and told me what to say and, more importantly, what not to say at the press conference. After they were satisfied I knew my role, it was back to the government sedan for the short drive back to the airport terminal building.

The two FBI agents escorted me into the Captain's Lounge, and Agent Smith asked me one more time if I knew where to go and what to say. I gave him my assurances and explained, "I made it from New York to Key West following navigational charts and bad weather—I think I can navigate a press conference." He gave me a blank stare and let me go.

When I stood up in front of the room, however, I felt more than a little nervous. More media people than I'd ever seen were packed into the room. What seemed like twenty microphones had been wired to the podium I now found myself behind. Flashbulbs were going off all over the place, and reporters from newspapers, magazines, radio stations, and television networks shot a barrage of questions at me. The first thing I did was make a brief statement saying, in essence, that I had not been mistreated and that the whole ordeal made me appreciate being an American like never before. I took a number of questions and managed to make the press corps laugh more than once.

One reporter asked me, "Hey, Fritz, did you know you were singled out by Fidel Castro and called a revolutionary?"

"What are you talking about?" I shot back. I couldn't believe what he was saying, and it was a little unnerving to think Castro had referred to me personally to preemptively discredit me.

I listened in disbelief, not knowing how to respond, when the reporter continued, "We monitored a speech he gave about the exchange, and he said you claimed to be an adventure-seeker paddling a canoe, but he said he knew you were really a revolutionary and a worthless character and that no one should believe the stories you would start fabricating. Castro said you were afraid you were going to be shot by a firing squad, but you had a letter in Spanish from your Senator that saved you. Did you have any such letter?"

At this point, Agent Smith stepped to the microphone and put an end to this line of questions, declaring, "Fritz cannot comment on this situation at the present time. Let's move on to something else."

I have no idea how long the press conference lasted, but I was able to wrap things up just in time to make a flight that had been arranged for me to Allentown. I was going home at last.

I couldn't escape the press, though. When I deplaned and walked into the lobby of the ABE airport late the same evening, the local papers and radio hosts wanted to ask me about my ordeal, too. And they weren't alone. A group of onlookers and, to my surprise, a high school band had turned out to greet me. I quickly either answered or deflected the questions tossed at me and then found my way outside the terminal, where I met one of my friends, who drove me to the Ale House. I had to thank Norman for all of his help. And boy, did I need a drink!

When I finally arrived at the Ale House it was a little past 12:00 midnight. I walked inside, and to my amazement the place was packed. I looked around; it seemed like everyone I ever knew was in that room. Then something caught my eye. The one wall was totally covered with news clippings, pictures, and stories from all over the world about "Fearless Fritz" and his wrongful imprisonment in Cuba. The jukebox was blaring, and apparently it was playing a song someone had written about me. I was standing at the bar feeling like I was really someone, dumbfounded, when all of a sudden even more people jumped out from back in the kitchen yelling, "Surprise!" with a Welcome Home cake.

Norman was the first to reach me, taking me in a quick embrace and shaking my hand. Andy Perkin came up to me next, all smiles and happy to see me.

But my biggest surprise was Julie. Her smile lit up her entire face when she threw her arms around my neck and welcomed me home with a huge kiss, to the cheers of the entire crowd. Drinks and food began to flow out of the Ale House's kitchen, and my friends took me to a seat of honor at one of his biggest tables. I told them all about my capture, my trial, and especially the watch story.

- "You're going to try it again, aren't you?" -

The party lasted for hours, and I was filled with a wonderful feeling of joy now that I was able to spend time with my "family" at home again. Finally it began to wind down as Norman's clock struck 4:00 a.m. When everybody else had gone, only Norman, Andy, Julie, and I were left. I drank the last sip of my beer, and Norman was glowing at me. I looked at him and returned his look of warmth. Julie looked back and forth at the two of us and sighed. Then she turned to me at last.

"You're going to try it again, aren't you?" she asked, smirking knowingly. I gave her a kiss and squeezed her hand.

"I need to finish what I started. Besides, what the hell else am I going to do around here? Honestly—no bullets, no flying watches, no thirty-five-foot waves? It's kind of dull, if you ask me."

Everybody laughed. I sat at the bar for a while, pinched myself, and soaked up the joy of the moment, knowing I was a free man in a free country and lucky to be alive.

Chapter 16: **The Final Attempt**

I did not return to the Gulf of Mexico for six months after my release from Cuba. During this time I was treated like royalty in Allentown. Any restaurant I walked into fed me for free. Norman swore up and down I could drink at the Ale House for free forever. Julie took a job in Allentown so she could stay nearby.

With no permanent place to stay, I found places to crash and get cleaned up besides the basement of the dry cleaners (which Norman also managed) adjoining the Ale House on the left. Sometimes it was at Julie's or Davies' or Andy's or Steve's place—and the list could go on. It seemed like I had my clothes all over Allentown.

- Reds came through -

Once I remember sleeping all night on a park bench across the street from the Ale House. The next morning I was awakened by Reds, the owner of the Sunoco station next door to the Ale House on the right. Reds was a good friend of Norman's.

I found out later that his name was Charlie Kemmerer, but I only ever knew him as Reds. And, believe me, that morning his face and temper matched his red hair—which is how, I figured, he got his nickname. He was livid when he found me, because what I had done was tear down the Sunoco banners hanging in front of the service station to use as blankets. It was all I could find to wrap around me. I was cold, tired, and not exactly in my right mind.

After he calmed down a bit, Reds came through like the generous, good-hearted man he was. Alongside his station, a wrecked 1969 Ford LTD with a big back seat had found a final parking space to serve as a parts donor. Reds gave me an extra set of keys to the Ford to use if I ever needed a place to sleep. It was a lifesaver for the next couple of months. I will always be grateful for Reds.

I appeared on TV and radio talk shows and gave lectures on the poor treatment of Americans in Cuba. Regardless of their status as a criminal or a refugee or something in between, I felt strongly that they deserved to be treated better, and I made it my cause. The bottom line for Fidel Castro became clear to me: he took over the island country by becoming the revolutionary leader of a band of revolutionaries, and he was not about to lose his grip on the nation to another group of new, different revolutionaries, especially not, as he viewed them, a bunch of Americans sent to Cuba by the CIA.

I came to realize for myself it was important to say nothing bad about any of the people I met while in Cuba for fear I might trigger even harsher treatment for them or ruin the little communication already opening up.

More than once, when I crossed paths with the federal government—especially when I talked about Cuba—it was clear FBI Agents Johnson and Smith were still keeping tabs on me. And I also remember a few people commenting on how few hijackings made the news anymore.

- *The wrong way* -

When I finally did get back to the Gulf, it didn't happen the way I'd hoped it would. My plan had been for the *Miss Allentown* and my equipment to be shipped to Mexico or a Central American country from which I could continue the second half of my voyage. Instead, everything ended up in the Bahamas. Dewar's, who had learned how much I enjoyed their Scotch by talking with Norman and by listening to my anecdotes along the trip, contacted me and offered to help sponsor me. I flew to Nassau on their dime and was their guest for a week at the Sailboat Club.

While I was at the club, I met some very friendly party girls from Pittsburgh, Pennsylvania. We had some wild times, but to paraphrase the popular saying about Las Vegas, what happened in Nassau will stay in Nassau.

It was a beautiful day when I finally got all my gear together and prepared to depart from Nassau. As I was saying good-bye, a friend of Norman's gave me some American "tobacco" to trade down in the islands. This surprise gift got me into almost as much trouble as my little unplanned excursion to Cuba!

The import/export inspectors decided to check out the *Miss Allentown* as I shipped out of Nassau, and I suddenly found myself summarily tossed in jail for marijuana possession!

After I was released following this little misunderstanding (the gift really was just tobacco), I restarted my trip south. I planned to travel south along the Bahaman Islands on my way to the Dominican Republic and from there to Puerto Rico and the Virgin Islands. It was easy in the beginning because the islands were close together. But as I paddled farther south, I discovered the islands were larger and farther apart. After Acklins Island, things became complicated.

Right after passing Acklins Island in the Bahamas, I was overtaken by a houseboat speeding around the south end of the island. The idiots narrowly missed running over me, and the wake of their boat swamped my little canoe. Trying to collect some of my supplies now washed overboard and floating around me in the water, I saw three naked girls jump into the water to offer me help. The boat had stopped when the captain saw what he had done to my little canoe. When we got everything together on the beach, they showered me with apologies for the mishap and invited me to board their houseboat. I naïvely accepted the invitation, and after we all got to know each other, I told them about my journey and my unscheduled trip to Cuba, and we soon became good friends.

I spent most of the morning on their boat while my things dried out. Slowly but surely, I began to realize who these people were and what was going on. On my tour of their boat they showed me four fifty-five-gallon drums of marijuana they were planning to smuggle from Jamaica to Miami. They had "run into me" while hiding and taking a little rest and recreation from their drug run. When I saw the grass, I quickly thanked them for their hospitality and made a swift exit to my canoe to continue *my* run for San Francisco.

Leaving these troubles behind, I felt happy-go-lucky again now that I had escaped another run-in with the law and was once again on my way. Did I actually say lucky? In reality, paddling the long stretches from island to island was now becoming harder and harder, reminding me of what had happened to my strength when I tried to cross the Gulf of Mexico the first time and fought the mighty Gulf Stream.

One day in this leg of the journey, I think somewhere near Turks Island, I came upon something really strange. It happened in the afternoon. All of a sudden I felt as if I had paddled into a vacuum chamber or a tube of some kind. The water became very calm, and there were no clouds. Now, I had witnessed scenes similar to this before, where the horizon seems to disappear when I'm very low in the water in my canoe and I can't tell where the sky ends and the water begins. But this was totally different. I felt as if I had wandered into a bubble. Everything was now the same color, and all my surroundings seemed to blend together. I felt as if I were floating in air. Then, in an instant, I saw what appeared to be a solid wall of fog.

- In the Bermuda Triangle -

This gave me an immediate flashback to the first day of my trip when I had left Staten Island and become engulfed by the fog on Hudson Bay. This column of vapor was not the same, though, because it was silent—there were no noisy ships' diesels, foghorns, or bells, and there were no car horns on nearby roads. This was a bright wall of fog, not a cloud. I couldn't estimate how wide it was, but I could see right and left very clearly. The whole column of fog glowed white, and there was fine, white foam all around my canoe. I can remember looking at this hedge of mist and almost identifying faces and objects, the way you can sometimes make out things when you look up at clouds in the sky. I can't say exactly how long this weird experience lasted, but then, suddenly, it was gone in a flash!

It took a long time for my heart rate to slow down after this encounter. After awhile I moved on, realizing I had somehow survived and emerged from the "Twilight Zone" of the glowing fog, and now faced the next big leg of my journey. I continued across a sixty-mile stretch from the Bahamas to Haiti and Hispaniola, a course dangerously close to Cuba.

It was during this stretch I noticed water was slowly seeping into my canoe and collecting at my feet. Even in good weather, I found myself bailing it out. To find out what might be wrong, during one of my swim times, I took the time to dive underwater and look closely beneath the *Miss Allentown*. I discovered that my new canoe, guaranteed by Grumman "for life" (I wondered if this meant my life or the canoe's), had a hairline crack across the bottom, caused probably by the continuous flexing of the aluminum in the ocean waves.

So here I was in trouble again—my boat was filling with water. For another thirty-two-hour stint at sea, I bailed water and tried to think about my true goals. Finally a sailing crew out of Key Largo, Florida, going to San Juan, Puerto Rico, found me, picked me up and took me in the direction of Cape Haitien.

Captain Jack, the owner of the boat, and his crew of six had already heard of me, and we talked for hours about Cuba and my trip. I also told them of my recent encounter with the bright fog. Captain Jack was more amused than surprised when he heard this story. He informed me that I was now in the Bermuda Triangle where many mysterious things were always happening to boats and planes.

I couldn't sleep that night. I kept asking myself if this was what those missing pilots and sailors saw right before their vessels disappeared inexplicably. Could I be one of the lucky few that had seen the wall of glowing fog and survived to tell about it?

When we finally arrived in Haiti, Captain Jack made certain I was able to get in touch with my contacts in the United States. There, with the assistance of some missionaries to whom Captain Jack had introduced me, I was able to contact Norman and tell him what had happened to the canoe. He told me to sit tight for a while until he could make some calls and figure out what to do next.

- No guarantee from Grumman -

A few days later, he got back to me with some bad news. Grumman, it turned out, would not honor its lifetime guarantee on the canoe, arguing it was not supposed to be used in open ocean waters! Norman consoled me, told me it was not worth pursuing a claim against the manufacturer, and said I should come home the best way I could find. I gave the boat and most of the equipment to the missionaries who had befriended me, and they were very thankful for my gift.

Reflecting on my latest failure, I became disgusted by the fact that four times I'd tried to attempt this voyage, and four times I'd lost everything! I had to face reality and give up trying to complete my ambitious adventure.

- Kicking myself -

I was able to ask for and catch a lift back to Miami on a cruise ship docked in Port Haitien, one of its stops on a route back north to Miami, thanks to the kind people at Dewar's. The captain of the ship remembered seeing me on television and invited me on board, where I was considered a "Guest of the Ship." I traveled first class, a far cry from paddling in a canoe.

One morning, standing on the quarterdeck of the ship, looking out across the desolate open waters of the Atlantic Ocean, I finally comprehended how a sane person would react upon spotting someone out in these waters trying to guide a canoe. I mentally kicked myself in the rear and said out loud, "I must be a complete idiot!" Fortunately, no one was close enough to hear me, or they might have believed what I had just yelled.

While this was the end of my adventures on the ocean, other exploits were already beginning to take shape in my mind. I could see canoes would figure in my future, as would a certain snowmobile. I knew I'd see Julie again, and I knew I could continue to count on support from Norman. But later that afternoon, while outside enjoying the fragrance of a gentle ocean breeze, knowing I'd nearly killed myself over an idiotic dare, I felt like everything, including my story, was at an end.

Once again, however, I had no idea how wrong I was.

Another dare, another time…?

Epilogue

When I look back over this adventure, I am amazed as I recall the many incredible things in my life I did in response to dares. And if you enjoyed meeting the people and hearing the stories that popped up at all the twists and turns of this canoe trip, you will be happy to know I will soon be giving sequels in the DARE series to my publisher. I certainly have a lifetime of stories to tell; far too many for one book.

My next book will take you on what I believe, in retrospect, was the most challenging adventure of them all: Once you've dried off from this DARE, we will embark together on a coast-to-coast adventure on a snowmobile from Westport, Washington, to Eastport, Maine, all on U.S. soil. Then, when you thaw out from that DARE, I will take you on a second waterlogged adventure across the northern United States in another canoe, using every waterway I can find, trekking from Portland, Oregon, to New York City, New York.

After my restlessness had mellowed some years following my release from Cuba, I described my adventures to a friend as "things that just happened." In retrospect, I'm not sure if I then went through a depression or just had a few soulful wrestling matches with my conscience, but I had very unsettling memories. I often say that what youth takes from us in stupidity, age usually gives back to us in wisdom. Some of this wisdom has helped me achieve a lot of personal growth. I was able to break free of alcohol in 1975 and from nicotine in 1985, which I am sure has added good health and years to my life.

But then I began to wonder whether maybe, just maybe, something or someone had been intervening on my behalf. How else could I have gone through so much turmoil and treachery and lived to tell about it? I did indeed live to tell about it … but why?

In 2006, I encountered the reason. I rediscovered my faith and with it gained a new perspective on my life. When I sought after God and asked the big questions, I learned that he saw worth in me. Why else would God save someone like me after I charged into such precarious situations and then failed to keep in touch with so many of the good, supportive people who were so very near and dear to me? My heart now aches for them, and I yearn to thank and apologize to a lot of people.

One such person is a devoted woman, "Julie," who was there for me through it all, yet I didn't realize her value at the time. This may have left her hurt and empty. I certainly know what it feels like to be hurt and empty, but I now also know unconditional love through God. I pray God is holding her and all my other good friends in His everlasting arms and that they feel the love I may not have given back. But giving back is what I feel I am being drawn to do.

My story never really meant anything to me until I met God. I realized how little it was about me and how much I had to write these stories for those around me, to share with everyone that what I thought was so important in my life turned out to be not so important after all. It is my hope that, having read *Adventure on a DARE,* you will share with others how one man has seen and done so much and come away unscathed so many times, finally to discover the reason behind it all.

It is my further hope you will also take the time to share your own adventure stories, as well as the quests you still wish to pursue, with the circle of people in your life. What better time to pause and give thanks to God?

I am honored to tell my amazing story. With humble gratitude for a newfound faith, I am Fritz T. Sprandel. Thank you, Lord!

Ode to Fritz

Adventurer, canoeist, bold was he,
Daring life for all to see.
A man of grit and focused way,
And true to task, he'd always stay.
No care for danger, risk or threat,
A chance he'd take to win a bet.
This man would gamble nature's call,
To prove his point or take a fall.
Yet days were chancy, fun and fast,
His reputation soon was cast.

But as the years went quickly by,
This man of quest sought questions, why.
Good friends had passed, left marks to bear,
Yet he remained with thoughts of care.
What was this man's true destiny?
And what was all life meant to be?
So, seek he did, in great detail,
For Godly word that couldn't fail.
And finding Christ, now saved was he,
Thus, spirit-filled for all to see.

Reborn now, Fritz fills his days,
In thanks for God's providing ways.
His life a script of saving grace,
Estranged paths, God did replace.
His quest now shines of telling all,
Of truth and love and Godly call.
Of walking paths the Lord will show,
And knowing life will surely grow.
That finding Christ was destiny,
And knowing God was meant to be.

Stephen J. Bell
© 07/25/07